MANAGING THE MUNCHIES:

A Celebration of the Phenomenal Fare of
Humboldt County, California

by Nancy Only

Photos by Matthew Filar

Creyr Publishing Inc.
Eureka, California
"Sharing the North Coast with the rest of the World."

MANAGING THE MUNCHIES:
A Celebration of the Phenomenal Fare
of Humboldt County, California
by Nancy Only
Photos by Matthew Filar

Copyright 2005

Printed in the United States of America
By Eureka Printing Company, Inc.

ISBN 0-9763594-2-1

ACKNOWLEDGMENTS

I've discovered that people in the business of feeding other people may just possibly be among the busiest people on the planet. To everyone who carved out time for me on this project, my deepest gratitude. Especially to those dear chefs who showed up on my doorstep with recipes in hand - you know who you are - endless thanks for your generosity.

To Pacific Flavors Cooking School, to Betty Burton, and to Micah Church, many thanks for helping me make elusive connections.

To The Great Intenders, without whom I'd have been in way over my head, my love and an enormous IOU.

To the friends and family who put up with my lack of availability, my heartfelt thanks for your patience, your faith and your support.

To *The Eureka Reporter*, and especially Glenn Franco Simmons, for allowing me to extend my love for the phenomenal fare of Humboldt County, please know how much I appreciate what you're doing, and how honored I feel to participate.

And to Matthew Filar, who so beautifully captures my vision of this wonderful area on film, there does not seem to be a vocabulary to express how much I treasure your interest, your artistry and your immense kindness, but I'm working on it.

Finally and most of all, to Roy, a creative genius in his own right who understood, put up with me and actively supported my commitment to this project: "Backatcha, Babe!"

Gentle Reader –

Surely you understand that things change and sometimes, in the process, chefs and restaurants come and go. Every attempt has been made to assure the information presented here is current. I cannot, however, guarantee that by the time it reaches you, it will still be accurate.

Nonetheless, please be assured the dining in Humboldt County will always offer remarkable rewards. The food here, and incredibly creative people who prepare it, are a tradition unlikely to change.

With Love –

Nancy Only

Fishing, Freshwater Lagoon   © *Matthew Filar*

Menu

Preface

When Archimedes realized he had discovered a way to move water uphill, he reputedly streaked through the streets of Syracuse shouting, "Eureka!"

Many centuries later at Sutter's Mill in northern California, James Marshall discovered gold, and "Eureka!" rang out again.

Today, visitors to Humboldt County report feeling that same sense of discovery when they stumble onto the beauty and the bounty behind the Redwood Curtain.

Perhaps it's the isolation. Three hundred miles north of San Francisco and one hundred miles south of the Oregon border, Humboldt boasts a single part-time freeway, US 101, running north and south, and two state highways running east and west. In rare times of natural disaster it is possible for the county to be completely cut off from the outside world.

Additionally, there is a sense of independence prevalent among the locals. In November, 1941, representatives from Humboldt County joined with those from seven other counties in northern California and southern Oregon in an attempt to secede from those two states. Weary of empty promises by politicians in Salem and Sacramento, the group urged their friends and neighbors to join them in the formation of the State of Jefferson. Weeks later, the bombing of Pearl Harbor derailed the movement, but the concept still lingers in the minds and hearts of local residents, and at least one current media ad makes notable reference to "the Humboldt Nation." As a result of the isolation, residents have developed a collective creativity that entertains and supports them.

Perhaps it's the natural beauty. Certainly the awesome Pacific Ocean on the west, the six rivers intersecting the land, the majestic redwood forests throughout, and the pastoral vistas of vineyards, dairy lands and produce farms dotting the landscape, merge to feed one's spirit with a rare and welcoming generosity.

Perhaps it's the climate. Along the coast the weather remains nurturingly temperate with magical, mystical fogs. Inland, warm summers and snow-draped winters produce a thriving agriculture and vast recreational opportunities.

These are the broad strokes. If it's true, as Flaubert noted, that God is in the details, then the county's remarkable creative output needs volumes to explain it. Additionally, it needs to be noted that restaurants and chefs come and go.

While every effort has been made to assure that the information in this volume is current as the book goes to print, tomorrow will certainly bring changes. But three facts which have stood the test of time emerge for our purposes here:

1. Humboldt County boasts a wealth of excellent indigenous foods.
2. The residents radiate inventive genius.
3. A primary demonstration of this genius can be found in the way we eat.

Dragboat, Pulp Mill; Humboldt Bay   © *Matthew Filar*

CHAPTER ONE

FISH

Many generations ago, the Original Tenants along the Klamath River had only nuts and berries to eat – a diet that left them unsatisfied much of the time. Rumors of salmon circulated, wondrous fish to absolve their hunger. But all the salmon were possessed by a pair of young women who lived where the Klamath and Trinity Rivers joined, and those young women would tell no one where the fish were kept.

Coyote, always the trickster, reasoned that he could unravel the secret and enjoy the bounty. He plotted to convince the maidens that he had salmon of his own. This, he believed, would motivate them to check their supply and determine if he had robbed them. He would follow them when they investigated and thus discover the source for himself. He found a piece of alder bark which he carved into the likeness of a fish. Then he covered his carving with deer fat that would sizzle realistically when the "fish" was grilled. Thus prepared, he went to the home of the young women, timing his arrival to coincide with the end of their evening meal.

With carefully chosen words, he lured them: "I see you have already finished your dinner, but your fire is still good for cooking. Might I please cook my dinner – a fine salmon which I have brought – over your fire?"

The maidens, nervous at his announcement, agreed. They watched uneasily as his "salmon" dripped its fat onto the fire. They watched as he appeared to hungrily gulp down his meal. They continued to watch as he pretended to fall asleep by the remaining embers. At last, convinced that he slept soundly, they tiptoed away to their secret stash.

Arriving at their fish-trap, they enjoyed tremendous relief. It remained secure, its contents still intact. They congratulated each other on being so clever, and went back to their home unaware that the cunning coyote had followed them.

Coyote ran to the fish-trap and yanked off the lid to get to his real dinner. The salmon leapt at the chance for freedom and escaped into the Klamath River. They remain there still, available now to everyone.

- Traditional Yurok Legend

North Coast residents have always eaten well. Hunters and gatherers, the tribes of the region found their dietary needs amply met. As with many of the American Indians, acorns were a staple here, and the forests of the region provided generously. Acorns were stored in baskets, leeched in other baskets, ground and then cooked in other baskets still. Indeed, basketry may have been the first of many local arts, and the work of local basket makers is highly prized among knowledgeable collectors.

Today it would be a challenge to find acorns on any menu or supermarket shelf, but other indigenous foods remain both popular and plentiful. Berries, especially blackberries, thrive to such an extent that they have become a bane for local gardeners. Tiny Trinidad hosts an annual Blackberry Festival to celebrate the prolific (or pernicious, depending on your taste in landscapes) plant, and blackberry cobblers, pies, jams and jellies mark the menus of local restaurants and specialty shops.

Forests also provided game – notably deer, elk and rabbit. Yet the waterways, the ocean, bays and rivers, offered the real wealth. Seaweed, sea lions, eels, shellfish, and steelhead, (even an occasional stranded whale) helped form a varied, balanced diet.

But salmon was king.

Salmon was a special blessing from The Creator. The annual First Salmon Ceremony, held in the early spring, was a ten-day event followed by a ten-day retreat, and was the only harvest festival celebrated by the Karuk people. They maintained an absolute taboo against eating, even touching fresh fish before the event, and believed that violating this sacred rule would cause the world to "fall apart." Special songs and prayers accompanied the catching of salmon, and at least one estimate suggests that a single family might consume up to two thousand pounds of it over the course of a year.

Traditional preparation of salmon works like this: Dig a shallow, oblong pit in the earth (or in the sand if you are on a beach), and start a fire of alder wood in the center. As the fire burns down to hot coals, filet an unskinned, very fresh whole salmon into a dozen or more steaks. At this point today, the steaks are liberally seasoned with salt and pepper.

Using redwood sticks a yard long and about an inch wide, thread several steaks onto each stick, running the stick between the skin and the flesh. Stand the sticks around the pit just out of reach of the fire, rotating them to obtain even cooking, until the skin is crisp – usually forty-five minutes to an hour.

Salmon feasts using this method take place each year throughout the county, and the public is invited to many of them. But twenty-first century technology has entered the picture in at least one instance. On the Hoopa Reservation, in the heart of Big Foot country, Hupa tribal members Leland Jordan and Carmeli Begay have joined with Yurok tribesmen Larry Jordan and John Biondini to form the Hoopa Processing Corporation. There they smoke and can wild salmon using the traditional recipe in updated form.

"For years I've been catching them, smoking them, and just giving them away," says Larry Jordan. "Then it occurred to me that I might be able to turn it into something more. I have a friend up in Gold Beach, Oregon, who started a cannery. I called him one afternoon to talk to him about it. He said, 'Why don't you come on up here and take a look at our operation?' So a bunch of us piled into the van and took off for Gold Beach.

"We got started in 2001, but the whole first year was spent in construction." The result of their efforts, a small but highly efficient cannery, makes use of what they learned from their Oregon contact. 'For example," Jordan continues, "he said 'You need a lot of tapered floor.' So when we went to work, we built that in. The concrete floors in the workrooms taper down to central drains. This means we can use hoses to wash the floors down. It really helps to speed the clean-up process."

The two Jordan men catch all the fish themselves – over three hundred of them a year. Larry Jordan has a full-time position in the Redi-Mix section of the Hoopa Roads Department, and his brother serves on the Hoopa Tribal Business Council, so they use weekends and vacations to fish. Each fish is filleted immediately and packed in ice. By the time they get it to the cannery, the meat has already cooled to 35 degrees. Before smoking, each filet is salted and peppered. Then a twenty-four hour period gives the naturally full flavor time to emerge. Next, in the centuries old tradition, the flesh is smoked with alder wood to create an authentic taste.

Some time back, the Jordans were given a sawmill which had fallen into disrepair. They went to work, got it up and running, and now use it to convert dried alder logs into the chips they use in a large contemporary smoker. Each load in the smoker yields two batches; ninety cans each, of finished product.

Begay describes the rest of the process: "Once we've smoked the fish, we cut the filets into strips and pack the strips into cans. We weigh each can, adjust the contents to make sure each one weighs exactly seven ounces, and wipe the can down. Then, one by one, we apply the lids, wipe the cans down again, and number them. We can tell you by that number when and where the fish in your can was caught.

"Next, we load the cans into retorts, pressure canners, where the temperature climbs to 253 degrees. We monitor the gauges continuously, and log the readings every ten minutes until the process runs its course."

"One thing I wasn't prepared for," Larry Jordan admits, "is how much work is involved in the marketing."

Begay agrees, explaining the cannery's special marketing challenge. "We do everything exactly to the FDA's specifications, but because we're on a reservation, we can't get the FDA to come out here and certify us. The federal government wants the state of California to deal with it, but the state won't touch it. And the markets won't put us on their shelves until we get certification. My father has already flown back to Washington, D.C., several times to try to get things straightened out.

"I've done some marketing in the Internet, and we've sold locally at craft fairs, but it's frustrating. We'd really like to expand, but right now we're sort of stuck."

The handsome label on the can states, "we hope that you will enjoy this delicacy as much as the generations of Native Americans have enjoyed the salmon resources from our rivers."

For years, families on the reservations have dried salmon and offered it as jerky. Now, thanks to the industrious efforts of the people at the Hoopa Processing Corporation, we can indulge the senses in moist smoked salmon off-season as well.

Of course, during the fishing season, county restaurants each offer their finest preparations of salmon and other locally caught fish. Mention seafood to old-timers in Humboldt County and their minds will leap to the name "Lazio." The family, with their cousins, the Aliotos emigrated to California from the Mediterranean in the nineteenth century. While the Aliotos settled in San Francisco, the Lazios came north to Eureka and grew from being commercial fishermen, to canning, marketing, and, ultimately, to running a popular restaurant.

Deborah Lazio went to work in her family's restaurant at the age of six, doing odd jobs in the business office. She graduated to the fish market on the premises, and eventually absorbed the full spectrum of restaurant-running lore. She speaks fondly of those days at the foot of Eureka's C Street where the Madaket now begins and ends its harbor cruises.

As a young woman in the 1980's, she stepped out on her own and opened the Old Town Bar and Grill. Although that site served no food, it showcased local musical talent and brought in well-known performers from outside the area as well.

Sometimes, in her off-hours, she frequented another local nightspot, the Jambalaya in nearby Arcata. "I actually met my husband on the Jambalaya dance floor," she says. "In fact, I think a lot of local couples first met there." That's not surprising; the dance floor was so notoriously small that everybody bumped into everybody else. Eventually she closed the Old Town Bar and Grill, but Jambalaya remained and continued to draw crowds on a regular basis.

In 1999 she and her husband, Jim Crawford, purchased Jambalaya, intending to add a restaurant to the bar. Working with Eureka architect, Jack Freeman, they began dismantling the structure. "We figured it would take three or four months," she says. "It ended up taking a year. The building was in dreadful shape. Together with the landlord, we actually ended up replacing the concrete foundation."

Jambalaya today is new from the ground up. Customers familiar with the former site feel as if they're entering another world when they walk through the door. Washed in sunny Mediterranean colors -- terra cotta and brown tiled floors with pale yellow walls -- the high-ceilinged room gives a surprising sensation of spaciousness. The dark-eyed, dark-haired owner looks right at home in her surroundings.

"We had planned to move the original bar to the opposite side of the room, but when we pulled it out, we found it had deteriorated badly. Jim teaches art at Humboldt State. He made this in his 'spare time'." She pats the surface of the sleek, terra cotta colored structure that now serves as a bar. Created of textured concrete, it has an almost silken finish. Behind it, alcoves, fitted with shelves and painted gold, house the bar stock and whimsical folk-art figures in bright hues.

On the walls, huge canvasses painted by Dimitri Mitsanas, also of Humboldt State's art department, add to the overall sophistication. A faux back wall of panels in airy textured ecru fabric can be moved to expand the dining room or curtain off a space for meetings, banquets or other large groups.

"Originally, we had a stage back there, but we found that live music didn't really fit in with the restaurant we had in mind. After a couple of years, I took out the stage, and we've been able to put this area to better use. I'm still involved with music in the annual Blues By The Bay Festival in Eureka, but it just didn't work for us here. Now we're able to focus on the food.

"We decided to retain the name 'Jambalaya' even though we knew newcomers might think of it as a Cajun restaurant. This place has been Jambalaya so long, and we've made so many changes, that we felt we wanted to keep the name. We do have our own version of jambalaya on the menu, but that's as far into Cajun territory as we go. Everything else is North Coast fresh.

"We do a Midnight Moon Primavera using Cypress Grove's newest chevre with chicken breast, seasonal vegetables and herbs over orecchiette pasta. And we offer an appetizer, 'Screaming Twins,' that won at the Oyster Festival. It's grilled oysters with a smoky chipotle aioli."

Also on the menu, Nonnie's Petrale Sole (baked in bread crumbs, asiago cheese, lemon beurre blanc and jasmine rice pilaf) comes from her own grandmother, who reigned as the Lazio family matriarch into her nineties, carrying on the tradition of creating recipes to bring out the finest flavors in northern California seafood.

Deborah takes a justifiable pride in what she and her husband have created. For example, at the front of the building, a demonstration kitchen fitted with a large window allows passersby to watch the cooks at work. Prep work still happens in the main kitchen, but they've worked out the logistics to create a smooth flow for the staff, diners and casual observers as well.

"We started out offering lunch and dinner seven days a week. It was too much. Now we serve dinner only, and only five nights a week. It's a much more realistic schedule, and much easier on the staff. We feel like it's the optimal arrangement for us to be able to do our best."

South of Eureka, the tiny village of King Salmon stretches along the shoreline, giving the residents of its small, flat-roofed homes, a splendid view of the bay. At the far end of the main street, Gill's by the Bay bases its bustling business on the words "simple" and "fresh." Open daily for breakfast and lunch, the restaurant focuses on seafood, and diners can enjoy a Hangtown fry, grilled crab sandwich, or blackened fillet of sole, as they watch fishing vessels work the bay.

At breakfast, homemade jam shows up on the table. "We may not have a wine cellar, but we do have a jelly room," jokes Denise Gill. "As much as possible, we make everything we serve from scratch. I don't understand why other places do it differently."

The building had been vacant for a decade when the Gills purchased it in 1990. Initially, they planned to demolish it and hold the waterfront property as an investment. But as they got into the job, they realized how solidly the building was constructed, and decided, instead, to remodel and reopen it. At the time, they were operating a dinner house at the nearby Whaler's Inn, so the breakfast-lunch combination fit well with their schedule.

In the intervening years, they sold Whaler's Inn and were able to devote their full attention on Gill's by the Bay. One enhancement they've added is a patio dining option.

Entering though a latticed gateway, customers encounter a broad expanse of deep green lawn bordered by roses, petunias and geraniums. The fiesta of color, extending to the umbrellas of the patio tables, strikes a bright contrast to the grayed blue-green of the bay itself.

Inside, large windows afford the same view. Photographs of fishermen with their prized catches cover the walls, further linking diners with their setting. Whether they park their car in the ample lot outside or tie their boats up at the nearby dock, guests at Gill's fully realize that this place exists because the bay exists.

To the Gills' credit, the staff has a long history with the restaurant. The cook started working there ten years ago, and the weekday waitress began just two months after they re-opened. The Gills, themselves, also wait tables and help out in the kitchen, giving a "family" feeling to the establishment.

Denise Gill relishes the fact that the bulk of their business is returning customers. "After a while, you get to know them by name, and they become friends. It makes the job a real pleasure."

Another gifted artist in the county's dining realm is chef Matt Szymanski whose first memory is of food. "I was at my grandmother's house in the high desert of southern California. She fed me a squash blossom. Years later, at a friend's house, I saw squash blossoms in the garden, and the memory came back full force. I could see my grandmother, sense her presence standing over me. I could see the squash blossom, smell it, even taste it. So I called my mother, had her give me my grandmother's recipe, and I made it. It was just like I remembered."

When he first left home, he worked in graphic arts and printing, joining his brother who had established a business in the Los Angeles area. "In those days, we worked with scissors and paste," he says. "Then computers came along. The money-making potential was huge, but the pace was overwhelming. I just didn't want to do it anymore."

Like so many others, he sought and found refuge in Humboldt County. "I'd never worked in a kitchen before. I showed up at Larrupin. They needed a dishwasher, and they hired me on the spot. It was graduation weekend, and the place was swamped. I walked into the kitchen, and it was like I was home."

He worked there for six years, then went to Portland. When he returned in 1994, he had gained experience and the conviction that cooking was his calling.

In 1998, he began formal education at The Culinary Institute of America in Hyde Park, New York. "It was classical training with a heavy emphasis on the French tradition," he explains with a smile that radiates enthusiasm.

When time came for him to do his externship, however, he returned to his grandmother's Italian heritage, and worked in Italy's Emilia Romana region. "It's world famous for its food – especially its cheese. That's where they produce Romano and Parmesan." In a leap of faith, he arrived there with no knowledge of the language and found himself at the bottom of the kitchen totem pole. But his boyish pleasure in recounting the experience indicates that the memory is a happy one.

Returning to Humboldt County once more, he ended up as chef at the nationally acclaimed Restaurant 301. "It was a major growth step for me," he says. "I'm so grateful to Mark Carter, the owner, for giving me the opportunity. I got to create the menus, run the kitchen and manage the staff. I'd done a lot of it before, but this is the first time I got to do it all. It's been terrific."

One of the things he appreciated in Europe was the use of fresh local ingredients in food preparation. Carter House, the Hotel Carter and 301 share gardens, which supply fruits, herbs and vegetables. Szymanski relates taking full advantage of them as well as the county's other indigenous offerings to create dishes such as seasonal vegetable risottos, wild salmon, and sautéed Pacific cod, changing the eight-course menu frequently according to the availability of ingredients.

It's turned out to be an ideal showcase for his style, which he describes as "not exotic". I use clean technique and clean presentation to produce simple, flavorful food. My foundation is Italian, and my training, heavily French. But local, seasonal ingredients always dictate the menu.

"My driving force is to get people back to the table. The Industrial Revolution has had a disastrous impact on the way we eat. I want people to learn again to respect where food comes from and all the things that go into it."

It's a noble ambition, but Szymanski appears to be well on his way to accomplishing it.

Without commercial fishermen, however, dining on the North Coast would lose a large claim to its fame. The men who brave the elements, cross the bar and bring home the catch are both the backbone and the unsung heroes of the process. Wayne Sohrokof is one such man.

Toward the end of his eight-year teaching career, Sohrokof and a co-worker began to share a fantasy: to take a year's leave of absence and go fishing. So when, in 1979, the opportunity to purchase a brand new boat presented itself, they turned in their resignations, boarded the fishing vessel *Drifter*, and never looked back.

The change proved dramatic. Where he once put in regular hours five days a week, with weekends, holidays and summers off, Sohrokof now finds himself at sea for six weeks at a time. "At sea, you're up at five- thirty, and you work straight through the day. You get to go to bed around ten p.m. because the fish don't bite at night."

His longest stretch ran forty-four days. "We were met by a ship that took on our catch and refueled us. We were fourteen hundred miles out, so it saved us a sixteen day turnaround."

Most of his runs are on the ocean. The *Drifter* works from Alaska to Mexico. In November, he goes after crab in San Francisco. When the crab season opens in Humboldt County in December, he works close to home, sometimes venturing north into Oregon and Washington. Summers, he trolls for albacore and fishes for halibut from southern California to Washington.

When the *Drifter* ties up away from home for any length of time, Sohrokof's wife Penny often flies to join him. The couple has built an extensive collection of photographs of the *Drifter*, detailing her journeys, catches, ports and crew members. Sorted into albums by year, each year begins with a photo of the crew, always labeled "the best crew ever." The photos offer an impressive overview and a compelling insight into why Sohrokof loves what he does despite the job's built-in variables.

Fishing is an unpredictable profession after all. Over the years, for example, the *Drifter*'s annual crab catch has ranged from fifteen thousand to over three hundred thousand pounds. The differences are due to many things: weather; plankton supply; events upstream. All these and more contribute to the success of a season. "It takes five to six years for a crab to mature," Sohrokof explains. "Any number of factors can interrupt the life cycle at any point during that time."

Occupational hazards also directly challenge the crew. Weather conditions like gale force winds, torrential rains, even ice storms punctuate Sohrokof's career. And he maintains that the greatest danger he regularly encounters comes each time he leaves and re-enters Humboldt Bay. Crossing the bar presents such peril that it initially prevented early explorers from settling the area, and seasoned pilots still exercise great caution in the process.

But none of these examples make up Sohrokof's chief concern. In his years on the *Drifter* he has seen repeated cutbacks at all fisheries brought about by government regulations. "The industry is in trouble," he says. "I'll be surprised if there *is* an industry in twenty years."

U.S. fishermen also face an overwhelming marketing problem. "None of the three major American fish canneries buys any tuna from American fishermen. American housewives want white meat, low fat tuna, older fish caught by long line or gill netting. Spain has opened a small market for us. They now buy about eight thousand pounds a year." His shrug speaks volumes. "We're becoming a dying breed. There are no young fishing boat owners."

After a moment, he regains his enthusiasm. "But we still look forward to starting over each year. Fishermen are eternal optimists."

NORTH COAST WAYS TO PREPARE FISH

Halibut is a favorite choice for North Coast cooks. It offers substantial fillets and lends itself to a wide variety of preparations. Here's a suggestion for a Creole-style entree.

Humboldt Halibut, Creole Style
   1 Tablespoon olive oil
   1 Tablespoon Dijon mustard
   1 teaspoon marjoram, dried
   1 teaspoon thyme, dried
   ½ teaspoon cayenne pepper
   1 ½ pounds Halibut fillet, cut into four equal portions
   fresh herbs and lemon wedges

   Mix oil, mustard, marjoram, thyme and cayenne. Rub lightly into the fish and chill 30 minutes.
   Preheat oven to 400 degrees F.
   Generously grease a baking sheet. Place fillets on this surface and place in the preheated oven for fifteen to twenty minutes, until fish flakes easily with a fork.
   Garnish with fresh herbs and lemon wedges and serve at once.
   (4 servings)

Prepare this with fresh ingredients, or use Hoopa Processing Corporation's Indian kippered Wild Salmon and fresh-frozen corn on short notice any time of the year.

Reservation Wild Salmon and Corn Chowder
  2 teaspoons extra virgin olive oil
  1/3 cup minced onion
  2 good-sized shallots, minced
  1 rib celery, finely chopped
  4 medium unpeeled red new potatoes, diced to ¼ inch
  salt and freshly ground black pepper to taste
  2 sprigs fresh thyme (or 2 teaspoons dried)
  1 and 1/3 cup heavy cream
  2½ cup stock (fish, vegetable or chicken)
  1 tablespoon butter
  8 chanterelles (or fresh mushrooms of your choice) sliced
  kernels stripped from 2 ears of corn
  1 7-ounce can Hoopa Indian kippered Wild Salmon
      (or ½ pound any good smoked salmon)

Heat oil over medium heat in a heavy saucepan. Add onion, shallots and celery and sauté until vegetables are translucent (about 25 minutes). Add potatoes and stir well to coat. Add salt and pepper, taste for seasonings and adjust as needed. Add cream, thyme and stock. Raise heat to medium-high and cook till potatoes are tender (15 - 20 minutes).

Melt butter in a skillet over medium-low heat. Add mushrooms and sauté until tender but not browned. Add to soup, along with corn. Cook five minutes.

Break up salmon, and add to soup. Heat through, stirring frequently, and serve. (4 servings)

When commercial fisherman Wayne Sohrokof has time at home, he and Penny enjoy entertaining. Their residence is ideal for outdoor functions, and Sohrokof usually has a supply of albacore on hand. This is a recipe he developed for just such occasions. It makes one and a half cups of sauce, but simple mathematics will easily double it, quadruple it, or more, depending on the size of your crowd.

Barbecued Albacore

    6 albacore fillets, 6 ounces each
    1/3 cup toasted sesame oil
    1/4 cup grated ginger
    1/3 cup fresh lime juice
    1/4 cup crushed garlic
    1/3 cup white wine
    2 Tablespoons soy sauce or tamari

Marinate the albacore fillets in the remaining ingredients for at least 15 minutes. Barbecue on a grill heated to medium temperature 15 minutes, or until fish flakes easily with a fork. Serve hot.
(6 serving portions).

Recipe courtesy of Wayne and Penny Sohrokof, FV Drifter, *Eureka*

Jeff Bronson has been both a fisherman and a cook for decades. He's also a rigorous critic. If Jeff says it's good, it's good. This, he swears, makes the best salmon he ever ate.

Jeff's Salmon Recipe
    1½ pounds salmon fillet cut into 2-inch wide strips
    Fresh cracked pepper
    Juice from ½ lemon
    6 cloves minced garlic
    1 bunch fresh cilantro, ground
    1 Tablespoon balsamic vinegar
    1 jar black caviar

Rinse the salmon and pat it dry. Pierce well with a fork and place in a glass dish.

Mix garlic, pepper and lemon juice and pour over the salmon. Refrigerate overnight.

Before cooking, allow salmon to come to room temperature. Bring a wood-fired grill to a medium heat.

Blend cilantro and vinegar. Set aside.

Drain the salmon and grill to desired doneness. Drizzle with cilantro-balsamic mix. Top each strip with ½ teaspoon black caviar and serve immediately.

(6 servings)

Recipe courtesy of Jeff Bronson, Fisherman and Cook-at-Large

Mike Vitiello, chef at Hurricane Kate's in Eureka's Old Town, is a master of sauces. This is just one of the ways he has created to dress grilled wild salmon.

Apricot Coconut Curry Sauce
> 3 Tablespoons ghee (clarified butter)
> 1/4 cup white onion diced to 1/4 inch bits
> 1 Tablespoon Garam Masala
> 1 teaspoon ground cinnamon
> ½ teaspoon ground cumin
> ¼ teaspoon cayenne
> 1 teaspoon white pepper
> ½ teaspoon salt
> 6 dried apricots, finely chopped
> 1 cup fish stock
> 1 can (14-16 ounces) coconut milk)
> optional garnishes: 2 tablespoons toasted coconut flakes
>   or 2 tablespoons sliced almonds

Place ghee and onion in a sauté pan over medium-low heat and sauté two minutes.

Add the spices and continue to sauté until the mixture becomes aromatic.

Add the apricots and stock and raise the heat to high. Cook, stirring continuously, until the sauce is reduced to 1/3 its original volume

Add the coconut milk and continue cooking until the sauce reaches your desired consistency.

Pour over freshly grilled salmon and garnish with toasted coconut flakes or sliced almonds as desired.

Recipe courtesy of Chef Mike Vitiello, Hurricane Kate's, Old Town, Eureka

The fresh fruit in this recipe creates unexpected flavors to perfectly compliment the lightness of the sole. It's simple to prepare, yet elegant enough to garner compliments.

Baked Petrale Sole with Fresh Fruits
   2 Tablespoons butter
   6 petrale sole fillets
   1 orange, thinly sliced
   1 cup seedless grapes, halved
   ½ cup Gewürztraminer wine
   ¼ teaspoon ground cloves

   Preheat oven to 400 degrees F.
   Melt butter in a baking pan at least 12" x 8". Swirl pan to coat bottom. Place sole fillets in pan in a single layer. Top each filet with an orange slice. Sprinkle grape halves evenly over all.
   Mix the wine and cloves. Add to the pan. Bake uncovered fifteen minutes. Serve immediately.
   (6 servings)

This recipe is somewhat complicated, but well worth the effort. You can substitute halibut, albacore, or any fish cut to ½ inch or more in thickness. When pressing down the edges of the pastry, press almost all the way through it to ensure a firm seal.

Salmon in Puff Pastry with Saffron Beurre Blanc and Asparagus Coulis

For the Asparagus Coulis
   1 ½ cups fresh asparagus tips
   1/4 cup heavy cream
   1 tablespoon salt

   Put the asparagus tips in a stainless steel pot with only enough water to cover them. Bring to a boil, then lower the heat and simmer until soft, but not over-cooked – about 12 to 15 minutes. Strain out the asparagus, reserving the liquid. In a blender, process the asparagus, cream and salt until smooth and thick, adding reserved cooking water as necessary. Chill.

For the Saffron Beurre Blanc
   2 cups white wine
   1/3 cup finely chopped shallots
   12-16 ounces (3 to 4 sticks) butter, cubed
   1 tablespoon fresh lemon juice
   1 teaspoon saffron threads
   ½ teaspoon white pepper
   1 to 2 teaspoons salt

   In a small stainless steel saucepan, melt 2 ounces of butter over medium-low heat. Add the shallots and cook until they are translucent. Add the lemon juice, white wine, saffron, and some of the salt. Bring the mix to a boil and then reduce heat and simmer until the liquid is reduced by 2/3. Reduce the heat to medium-low, and whisk the remaining cubed butter, a few cubes at a time, until the sauce is thick and creamy. Then whisk in the cream and white pepper.

Serve right away, or keep warm. (For aesthetic purposes, the beurre blanc may be strained through a fine sieve to remove any solid matter.)

For the Salmon in Puff Pastry
1 ½ pounds fresh salmon cut into 4-ounce portions
purchased puff pastry dough
1 egg thoroughly mixed with 1 tablespoon of milk
salt and pepper to taste
garnishes, as desired

Season salmon on all sides. Cut the puff pastry into 5"x 5" squares. Place a salmon portion on the corner of a pastry square. Brush the edges of the dough with egg wash. Fold the dough over the salmon to form a triangle. Using a fork, press edges together to seal. Brush the entire surface with egg wash. Bake at 400 degrees F for 15 to 20 minutes.

Presentation
Decorate the plate with Saffron Beurre Blanc, rotating the plate to cover. Arrange pastry on top of beurre blanc, and drizzle with the asparagus coulis. (Alex uses a squeeze bottle to achieve a decorative effect.) Sprinkle with minced red bell pepper, minced fresh parsley and/or other fresh herbs as desired.
(6 servings)

Recipe courtesy of Chef Alex Begovic, Personal Caterer, Eureka

Chef Paul Clarke selects ingredients with distinctive flavors which balance beautifully to make this a memorable delicacy.

Tuna Tartare
   8 ounces Sashimi grade Yellow fin tuna
   ½ ounce peanut oil
   1 lime
   1 bunch cilantro, roughly chopped
   wasabi powder (optional)
   salt and pepper to taste
   1 baguette good French bread
   ¼ cup melted butter
   4 Serrano chilies
   4 teaspoons roasted garlic, chopped
   4 teaspoons fresh ginger, chopped
   ½ cup toasted pine nuts
   1 bunch Thai basil, chiffonade

   Dice the tuna with a sharp knife to 1/4-inch bits. Work quickly to prevent tuna from getting warm. Cut cleanly. Do not mash or mince.

   Dress fish with peanut oil, juice from a lime, and chopped cilantro. If you want this really spicy, add a pinch of wasabi powder. Season with salt and pepper to taste. Chill no less than one hour, no more than four hours.

   Thinly slice the baguette diagonally. Brush with melted butter and toast in a 400 degree oven on both sides.

   Finely dice chilies. Using a ring mold, center tuna on a plate. Surround with chilies, garlic, ginger and pine nuts.

   (4 appetizer portions)

Recipe courtesy of Chef Paul Clarke, The Groves at Riverbend, Myers Flat

The pink peppercorns called for in this recipe are not truly a pepper, but a Haitian berry with a unique, lingering flavor. They can be found at most specialty food stores. The salmon can be encased in puff pastry earlier in the day, brought to room temperature and baked just before serving.

Halibut and Shrimp in Puff Pastry with Pink Peppercorn Beurre Blanc
    1 pound fresh Halibut fillet
    2 sheets puff pastry
    ice water
    4 large prawns, peeled, deveined, tails removed
    salt and pepper to taste
    6 to 8 ounces of butter, cubed
    3 tablespoons finely chopped shallots
    1 cup dry white wine
    1 ounce heavy cream
    1/4 tablespoon ground pink peppercorns
    1/4 tablespoon whole pink peppercorns

When ready to prepare, preheat oven to 450 degrees F. Cut halibut into four equal portions. Lay out a sheet of puff pastry. Brush it lightly with water. Place fillets on the pastry sheet. Top each fillet with a prawn. Season with salt and pepper. Cover with second puff pastry sheet. Press down with your fingers around each piece of fish to remove any air bubbles. Using a large cookie cutter or a sharp knife, cut out the dough around each fillet, leaving at least one inch all around each piece. Refrigerate immediately, or bake fifteen to twenty minutes, until golden and puffy.

In a small stainless steel saucepan, over medium heat, melt one tablespoon of the butter. Cook shallots, without browning, until translucent.

Add the white wine. Increase heat and bring to a boil. Allow to reduce to one third the original volume.

Add the remaining butter, a few cubes at a time, while whisking over medium-low heat, until the sauce is thick and creamy.

Add the pink peppercorns, salt and cream. Simmer over low heat a few more minutes and serve.

(4 entree servings)

Recipe courtesy of Alex Begovic, Chef and Personal Caterer, Eureka

Crab Pots © *Matthew Filar*

CHAPTER TWO

SHELLFISH

One Saturday in June differs from the other fifty-one during the year. By 10:00 A.M., workers have set up tables on the Arcata Plaza and dressed them in blue or white tablecloths. They wrap lamp posts, Maypole-style, in bright colors and join them at their tops with arches of dozens of white balloons. Farmers Market vendors move to the far side of the surrounding streets to make room for the brightly colored tents that ring the plaza proper. Huge grills begin to smoke while restaurateurs, caterers and civic organizations get ready to compete in the annual Arcata Bay Oyster Festival.

Conditions in Arcata Bay combine to create an ideal environment to ranch oysters. Over seventy percent of them grown in California come from a scant four hundred and fifty acres here. Culturers plant seed oysters in bags attached to poles. The poles, in turn, are sunk into the bay floor, and the crop spends about eighteen months maturing to harvest size. June, the high point of the harvest season, becomes the likely time to celebrate, and celebrate they do.

On this Saturday, chefs from all over the county reveal heretofore secret combinations of ingredients designed to enhance the experience of savoring these splendid bivalves. As many as ten thousand people crowd the plaza, and queue up at over forty stands, waiting good-naturedly for their share of the one hundred twenty thousand oysters served.

On the north side of the plaza, local radio station KHUM holds forth on stage with some of the best and most festive music by area performers, from Cajun, to reggae, to folk ballads, to jazz. While the music makes the wait pleasant, aromas from the many grills promise a payoff for patience, and the balmy, almost-summer weather typical of the North Coast in June, adds to the pleasure of consumers and servers alike.

Oyster lovers are passionate people – especially in their pursuit of the mollusk. And Humboldt County chefs cater to this passion in countless ways.

Posted menus at each outlet announce taste-tempters like oysters in kiwi, lime and ginger mignonette, Spanish barbecued oysters with smoked paprika, olive oil, onion, garlic and orange zest, or sambal coconut barbecued oysters with red bell pepper crème fraiche. One customer in line expressed a sentiment held by thousands when she said, "We wait three hundred and sixty four days every year for this, and it's always worth the wait".

In the midst of this bounty, the music stops temporarily to make room for the traditional Oyster Calling Contest. Participants as young as five and as old as –well, fully adult – take the stage with their renditions of sounds and songs to lure the bashful bi-valves. Individual interpretations evoke laughter and applause from the crowd and enhance the already festive feel of this very special celebration.

If you're squeamish, perhaps, or you just don't like oysters, the event offers other options. The Humboldt County Cattlemen's and Cattlewomen's Associations barbecue tri-tip steaks. May's Chinese Food, Annie's Cambodian Food, Lao Style Food and a hot dog stand all carry land-based comestibles. A cotton candy machine and Bon Boniere ice cream satisfy sweet teeth, while Fieldbrook Valley winery and local micro-breweries quench thirsts.

Betty Burton, hostess of "KINS Kitchen," a food related talk show on local radio, has judged the competition for nearly a decade. A lifetime in the entertainment industry at an international level, years of fine dining in restaurants around the globe, and a reputation as an excellent caterer qualify her for the job, which she declares a labor of love. Undaunted by the prospect of eating at least one oyster from each vendor, she actually looks forward to the experience. "I never met a food I didn't like," she says with a contagious laugh. "I love seeing what the various restaurants come up with. Many of the combinations are really ingenious and surprising."

She has watched the festival grow to its current proportions and rejoices at its success. Yet she speaks wistfully of some of the elaborate preparations in earlier years when the festival was smaller. "Savory Thyme Catering would use lots and lots of flowers, for instance. And I remember one year when Café Tomo served beautiful rice-lined seaweed cones with barely fried oysters spilling out. There were lots of shredded garnishes and lots of color. You could tell that the entrants lavished time on each individual oyster." Her favorite ways to eat oysters are either on the half shell or grilled just until the shells open, then served with salsa.

Hurricane Kate's, in Eureka's Old Town, has walked away with honors several years in a row, and Mike Vitiello has run the kitchen there since the restaurant opened. "I was working in Arizona in 1999 when Kate Chadwick called and offered me the job. She pulled her staff from a number of different places. She'd worked with each one of us before, and we were all excited at the prospect of working with her again. She's an amazing chef, and she has the phenomenal ability to create a family environment."

His dark eyes shine with intensity and enthusiasm as he shares what it's like to work with "The best staff ever." For him, it's one of the reasons he's been at this job longer than any other he's held. "There's a huge burn-out factor," he admits. "Usually I can do it about nine months and then I drop out and go back to being a line cook for a while."

But he feels a real investment at Kate's. "I helped this place get started. I painted this wall." He gestures to a vibrant burnt orange expanse displaying the work of a local artist. Hurricane Kate's is a site for Eureka's Arts Alive! Program, and exhibits paintings by a different artist each month. It's one of the many win-win situations Vitiello enjoys. The artists benefit from showing their work, and the restaurant benefits from the hordes of gallery crawlers who show up for the openings on the first Saturday of each month.

He gestures again, this time to the mottled concrete beneath him. "I helped seal this floor." The floor is a story all its own. The space the restaurant occupies once served as the parking garage for the historic Vance Hotel. Rather than cover it, Kate decided to play it up. They scrubbed it, but left the oil stains from years of parked vehicles, adding splashes of other chemicals to heighten the character, then sealing the whole. The effect perfectly complements the exposed pipes overhead, creating a fusion of urban chic and local history appropriate to a restaurant where the menu is a fusion of world-wide flavor and fresh local ingredients.

Those ingredients also inspire Vitiello's enthusiasm. He delights in the weekly Farmers Market half a block from his kitchen, and revels in his interaction with the young farmers – another win-win situation. He cites a recent exchange in which a grower gave him two pounds of purple tomatillos. Vitiello had never seen purple tomatillos, and the grower urged him to experiment with the unusual specimen, knowing the results would be shared, expanding the market and boosting future sales.

"I'm a desert boy. I've always been able to order any kind of produce or seafood, but this is different. To be able to get it from the hands that grew it.... That's something else.

"One of the things I learned was how to tell if a fish had been previously frozen. Inland, you need to know how to do that. Here, the seawater is practically still dripping from the gills.

"People show up at the back door with black chanterelles they've just picked and ask if I'll pay three dollars a pound for them. Yes, I could order them in Flagstaff or Austin – for maybe twenty-five dollars a pound - but I'd have to trust the supplier. This is a whole different world."

Conversation turns to the oyster festival where Kate's entries have consistently taken honors, and he grins broadly. "It's insane. This year our stand went through thirty-six hundred oysters. We started a week ahead gathering what we'd need. Then, that morning at five o'clock, a big truck pulled up to the back door and we all started loading it up. Everyone worked a double shift that day.   The night shift worked the early part of the day at the plaza. Then they came back here and the day shift went to Arcata and finished up there."

Discussing his staff once again, he expands on his appreciation of them. "We're getting ready now for an art exhibit. Every piece in it will be done by someone who works here. They're not just phenomenally dedicated; they're enormously creative, too.

"That young woman," he nods toward an attractive blond, "basically makes all my bases. I can say to her, 'Give me something with pineapple and cucumbers,' and I know she'll do it. I'll come back, and she'll say, 'Taste this,' and all I have to say is, 'More cumin' or 'Amp up the spices,' or 'That's great.' Anything you'd open a can or a jar to get, she creates fresh, from scratch, right here. And the guy standing next to her," he nods again, "does all the sauces for our oysters. We change them once a month, so he's always working on something new.

"I'm not saying it's always smooth. Sometimes we're really swamped, and I'll snap at someone, or someone will snap at me. But by the end of the evening, we're over it, and we'll all go out together to unwind. He reiterates, "Kate is the only chef I've ever wanted to work for this long. And this crew is more than a dream team. They're a real family."

Todd Lawson has also worked the Oyster Festival with success. His sandy hair, green eyes and youthful appearance might lead you to think he's a surfer rather than an award-winning chef. Yet he's been in the restaurant business since 1985, and put himself through Humboldt State University cooking. He holds a degree in environmental biology and, most recently, a position as chef at Dixie Gorrell's Larrupin Café outside of Trinidad.

He's worked at some of the brightest lights in North Coast dining: Carter House/301, Abruzzi, and five years at his own establishment, Celestino's in Eureka's Old Town. It seems appropriate that he would have found his way into Larrupin where memorable meals are the rule.

Based in a two-story house on rural Patrick's Point Drive, Larrupin serves meals on both floors in an elegant yet comfortable setting. The house menu has remained the same since 1986, but diners agree that the results are worth going back for again and again. It's a place for special celebrations, and the perfect spot to take out-of-town guests that you want to impress.

"It's a back-country rib room," Lawson insists. "They're the best ribs anywhere, and I don't even like ribs. But at Larrupin, they're delicious." He maintains that the location is back-country despite the fact that, for Humboldt County, Trinidad is definitely an upscale address. And he says that, in summer, even with the restaurant's reputation as a fine-dining house, guests arrive in shorts and tank tops, and are treated with the same respect as those who dressed up for an evening on the town.

Larrupin recently opened their new patio for *al fresco* dining. A second menu now affords more casual fare, and lower prices, for outdoor guests. That second menu is largely Todd's creation. "I learned a lot from the mesquite grill and the smokehouse there, too. For instance, I developed a scorched horseradish sauce that I think is pretty terrific. The charring seems to seal in the sugars and take away the burn. I like it a lot better than the regular sort."

His enthusiasm for his work expresses itself in many ways. For example, he considers working with the suppliers a definite perk. "They give me an idea of what's going to be available, what I can look forward to working with next. The big thing," he points out, "is FRESH. We have so much in this area that's good."

Amen, Todd, and amen, Larrupin. Thanks for showcasing the best behind the Redwood Curtain.

Billy Birks grew up in Eureka, but now, at twenty-four years old, he believes he had to leave it in order to fully appreciate it. During high school, he worked for a burger bar, and then for a seafood restaurant. Those experiences led him to want to learn more about food preparation, so after earning an Associate of Arts degree from College of the Redwoods, he enrolled at the California Culinary Institute in San Francisco.

"Looking back," he says, "I wish I'd had more cooking experience under my belt before I went. They were pretty much geared to teaching people who already knew the basics. But it opened a lot of doors for me."

The biggest of those doors was an externship in New York City at Windows on the World, once the nation's most profitable restaurant. "When my externship was up, they kept me on. I got to work every station in the kitchen except the sauté station. I was scheduled to work there next when the September eleventh tragedy happened."

With his job gone, Birks went to London where he worked briefly as a co-chef. But on a visit home, he applied for the *sous* chef position in the kitchen of Avalon, a new upscale restaurant in Eureka, and was hired. "Right now," he says, "I can't think of anything I'd rather be doing. The space, the menu, the staff are all really good. And, of course, I love to cook. I feel really lucky to be there."

He pauses briefly, reflecting, and then continues. "You know, it's funny.

My mother never cooked much. My sister and I were pretty much on our own where meals were concerned. Frozen burritos and macaroni-and-cheese formed the bulk of our diets. Somehow I always knew that there had to be more to it than that.

"My mother laughed when I told her what I wanted to do. But since I became a cook, she's grown exponentially in the kitchen."

What have been his motivating factors along the way? "I've learned a lot from the chefs I've been able to work with. I remember a chef at Windows on the World who told me that, for every piece of fish I overcooked, I'd have to do five push-ups. I think I did twenty-five push-ups that night, but I loved it. The discipline and structure were exactly what I needed."

Today he finds Avalon exactly what he needs to keep his career on track. The restaurant has recently hired a kitchen manager, which relieves the pressure of business details that plague many chefs. And he appreciates the opportunity to work with the seasonal changes in Humboldt County's available fare.

"We have incredible raw materials here. I actually get goose bumps when the mushroom foragers show up with their findings. The morels, the chanterelles, the shiitakes...." A shiver of delight runs over him as he describes it. "This county is one of the best spots in the world for wild mushrooms.

"The Farmers Markets, the seafood, and the dairy products...." His eyes widen. "Cypress Grove makes some of the most sought after chevre anywhere in the world, and it comes from little McKinleyville! It's hard to imagine, but it's true. We have first-rate food to offer here. It's a joy to be part of the process."

His long-term goals include opening a restaurant of his own. "I've still got a lot to learn before I do that," he admits. "I figure it's twenty or thirty years down the road. But I've already got a mental image of the kind of place I want. At California Culinary we had a class where we used software to design our ideal restaurant. And I've worked in enough restaurants now to know what works and what doesn't in terms of size, placement and logistics.

"Actually, Sunset Restaurant in Trinidad looks a lot like what I designed – big windows looking out over the Pacific, nice table linens, the works. And the kitchen at Avalon is pretty close to ideal the way it's laid out.

"I love what I'm doing, but I don't want people to get the idea that just because I work at an upscale restaurant I'm some hoity-toity chef. I like to prepare simple food, like lamb shanks or a nice *boeuf Bourguignonne*, but I want to prepare it so well that the people I'm cooking for love it. I'm basically a simple guy. I still eat macaroni-and-cheese."

Birks was in kindergarten in the 1970's when Scott Sterner came to Humboldt State University from Southern California. "I've always loved the ocean," he says. "That's why I chose Humboldt." It may also be the reason he majored in Fisheries as well.

"In those days, aquiculture was pretty much all about trout and salmon farming. But by the time I graduated, there were a couple of places developing single-seed oyster culture. One was down in Monterey. I didn't know anything about shellfish, but I thought it sounded interesting, so I went down and signed on with them.

"I worked there about six months, but there were some problems – mainly, I was making minimum wage, and housing in that area was pretty expensive. Eventually, I decided to head for Washington State to check out the options there.

"On the way, I came back through Humboldt County and connected with Ted Kuipper. I'd known Ted for years. He was just starting Pigeon Point Shellfish, and he offered me a place there. I worked for him from 1979 to 1981 when they closed. I bought some of their equipment, and took over the lease Ted had on some bay acreage, so I decided to stay here and go into business for myself."

North Bay Shellfish, the result of that decision, is still going strong, and manages to keep him hopping. "We harvest according to the tides, and of course the tides change daily – not only by time, but by depth as well. It means working day or night (which we call sunset cruises). It takes two or three days' work to harvest enough to meet our commitments to local restaurants and to the Farmers Markets. We're always looking ahead to see how we're going to be able to do it.

"Oysters grow at different rates during different times of the year. I've been able to get some wet storage in Mad River Slough, which helps a lot. I can pull bags that are ready to harvest and put them in wet storage. Then I can harvest them much more quickly and easily for restaurant deliveries on Wednesdays and Farmers Markets on Saturdays."

Currently, Sterner employs two systems of ranching the bi-valves. He buys small oysters, three-eighths to three quarters of an inch long, from seed producers to grow in bags in the bay. He also purchases oyster "larvae" from hatcheries. He sets the larvae on imitation shells attached to a line as long as fifty feet. The line will hold up to five hundred oysters, which grow in clumps on the shells. In roughly two and a half years, the oysters reach medium size "Those lines are really heavy by then," he says.

In many ways, Sterner finds the work rewarding. "I like being outdoors, and I like the independence of working for myself." But the business clearly comes with challenges. "There are always permits to deal with. And we're always working on water quality. That's essential if we're going to harvest a decent crop. It seems like I'm always juggling."

Sterner, the father of three, strives to make family time a high priority. He also works hard to assure that North Bay Shellfish offers a quality product. "We spend a lot of time sorting to assure uniform size, and our oysters are always really fresh. We harvest Friday afternoon or Friday evening for the Farmers Market on Saturday morning. You can't go to the supermarket and find them that fresh."

Perhaps his biggest frustration, though, comes from self-styled environmentalists. "I used to consider myself an environmentalist. We work hard to improve the water quality in the bay, for the business and for everybody else's good. Yet I often find myself coming under the gun from people who spend very little time, if any, on the water, and who draw their conclusions from dubious science."

In addition to Pacific, Kumamoto, European and Eastern oysters, North Bay Shellfish raises Manilla and soft-shelled clams and bay mussels when conditions permit. It's a year-round operation. Those who remember the old "Oysters 'R' In Season" signs in seafood restaurants no longer have to wait through summer months to enjoy the marvelous mollusks. In Humboldt County, fresh oysters are always in season.

NORTH COAST WAYS WITH SHELLFISH

For this bit of divinity, you'll need a dozen fresh oysters shucked and removed from their shells. Keep the bottom half of the shells and clean them with cold water, then place the oysters back in the half-shells and proceed with the following:

Oysters Au Gratin

Preheat oven to 450 degrees F.

For topping:

3 tablespoons melted butter

¼ cup freshly minced parsley

½ teaspoon finely grated lemon zest

1 cup bread crumbs

½ cup freshly grated Parmesan cheese

Mix all ingredients by hand until well blended. Set aside at room temperature.

For sauce:

2 tablespoons butter

1/4 cup finely chopped shallots

½ tablespoon ground garlic

1 cup champagne

1 cup heavy cream

3 teaspoons salt

In a large saucepan melt the butter over medium-low heat. Add the shallots and cook till soft, but not brown. Add the garlic and cook briefly, one to two minutes. Add the champagne and increase the heat to medium-high. Bring to a boil and reduce the sauce to 1/3 its original volume. Add the cream and bring to a simmer. Let the sauce thicken a few minutes, then add the salt.

Pour the sauce over the prepared oysters and sprinkle them with the crumb topping.

Bake in a heat-proof dish until golden brown. (4 servings)

Recipe courtesy of Alex Begovic, Premiere Personal Caterer

Betty Burton, who has traveled the world and explored food in innumerable sites, says, "With the wonderful fresh oysters in our area, I love to serve them raw or lightly cooked, to show off their sweet flavor. Simple is best. You can use whatever fresh oysters are available to you. I particularly like the smaller oyster for this presentation."

Oysters with a South-of-the-Border Kick

1 to 2 dozen Kumamoto oysters

Salsa:

1 ½ cups finely diced tomatoes (3 medium)
½ cup finely diced green onions (approximately 4)
1 jalapeno pepper, finely diced (remove seeds to tame fire)
1 tablespoon finely chopped cilantro
1 lime, juiced
splash of tequila (optional)

Mix salsa ingredients together

In a covered grill, place oysters over high, direct-heat coals. Cover and check after four or five minutes. The shells will pop open. Do not use any oysters that have not opened. Remove the top shell, and with a knife, cut through the attached bottom of the oyster to loosen.

To serve, arrange oysters on a platter with salsa on the side. If you use individual plates, top each of the oysters with salsa. A wedge of lime is a nice garnish with a bouquet of cilantro leaves. (18 to 24 oysters)

Recipe courtesy of Betty Burton, Esteemed Judge, Arcata Bay Oyster Festival

For this recipe, Burton specifies that she likes the Kumamoto oyster grown in Humboldt Bay, or our small Pacific oyster. The number of bi-valves you use in this preparation is determined only by the size and appetite of your crowd.

Marinated Oysters

    2 dozen to 3 dozen raw oysters
    ¾ cup extra virgin olive oil
    3/ cup canola oil
    2 medium onions, peeled and thinly sliced
    3 tablespoons red wine vinegar
    1 teaspoon salt
    ½ teaspoon freshly cracked black pepper
    1 teaspoon crushed red pepper (more if you like spice)
    lemon wedges for garnish

Put all ingredients, except for lemon wedges, in a tightly covered container. Marinate, chilled in the refrigerator.
Serve, garnished with lemon wedge (24 to 36 oysters)

Recipe courtesy of Betty Burton, Oyster Lover/Festival Judge

Local oysters are definitely one of the benefits of living here. Todd Lawson shares his take on our marvelous mollusks.

Oyster Pate
   24 oysters, freshly shucked
   5 slices hickory smoked bacon
   ½ red onion, chopped
   1 small red bell pepper, chopped
   3 cloves fresh garlic
   1 teaspoon Dijon mustard
   1/4 teaspoon crushed red pepper
   splash of brandy

In a 10-inch skillet over high heat, layer bacon, onion, bell pepper, garlic, mustard, red pepper and brandy. Cook on high flame until simmering well. Reduce flame to medium-low and simmer for ten minutes. Place all ingredients in a food processor and blend for five minutes. Place in a deep-sided ½ quart pan, cover with waxed paper, and refrigerate overnight.
   Serve with crostini and hard cheese.

Recipe courtesy of Todd Lawson, Multiple-Venue Chef, Humboldt County

Like many true oyster fanatics, Todd doesn't specify serving sizes on this recipe.
You know who you're serving. You decide.

Pancetta-Balsamic Butter Baste

Thin slices Pancetta
2 teaspoons finely diced shallots
1/4 teaspoon finely diced garlic
1/4 cup balsamic vinegar
1/4 cup water
2 tablespoons whole butter

In a sauce pan, cook pancetta until brown . Add shallots and garlic.
Cook 1 minute.

Deglaze pan with vinegar. Add water and reduce by one third.
Whisk in butter.

Use this sparingly on top of shucked oysters, either raw or broiled.
(Again, serving size depends on crowd size)

Recipe courtesy of Todd Lawson, Oyster Meister, Eureka

This isn't the festival's winning oyster preparation, but it is one of the many ways fresh oysters are served at Hurricane Kate's award-winning restaurant.

Fresh Tomato and Sambal Mignonette
    24 oysters on the half shell
    2 tablespoons minced shallots
    2 tablespoons red wine vinegar
    2 tablespoons dry sherry
    1 ½ tablespoons ice cold water
    3/8 teaspoon black pepper
    1/8 teaspoon white pepper
    1 ½ cups fresh seasonal tomatoes diced to 1/4 inch
    1/4 teaspoon sambal
    Vietnamese chili paste (optional)
    1 bunch fresh Thai basil leaves

    Mix shallots, vinegar, sherry, water and peppers.
    Let stand one hour.
    Add diced tomatoes and sambal. If you want a spicier flavor, add chili paste to taste. Blend thoroughly.
    Place 1/4 teaspoon of mixture on each oyster. Top each oyster with a leaf of Thai basil. (4 first course servings)

Recipe courtesy of Mike Vitiello, Hurricane Kate's, Eureka

To achieve a chiffonade, roll the nori sheets into a firm cylinder and slice across the cylinder to produce very narrow ribbons.

Humboldt Bay Kumamoto Oysters with Sake Mignonette

    18 kumamoto oysters, cleaned, shucked and returned to half of shell

    1 cup sake

    1 large shallot, finely chopped

    1 teaspoon freshly ground pepper

    1 tablespoon rice wine vinegar

    zest of 2 lemons

    2 sheets of nori paper, chiffonade

Arrange oysters on a platter of ice or salt.

Combine sake, shallot, pepper and vinegar, and let stand at least 15 minutes.

Spoon a teaspoon of the mignonette onto each oyster. Sprinkle with lemon zest and nori chiffonade.

Serve immediately. (18 oysters)

Recipe courtesy of Billy Birks, sous chef, Avalon, Eureka

Chowders are a tradition in coastal towns. This one is a flavorful improvement on the old-fashioned oyster stew.

Oyster and Sweet Corn Chowder
  30 Kumamoto oysters, cleaned and shucked
  2 pounds celery, cleaned, medium diced, and divided
  4 pounds onions, peeled, medium diced, and divided
  2 fresh bay leaves
  ½ bunch fresh thyme
  kernels from 4 ears sweet corn (reserve 2 cobs)
  water
  ½ pound bacon, finely diced
  1 large russet potato, peeled and diced to 1/4 inch
  1 quart heavy cream
  1 bunch fresh tarragon, finely chopped
  1 tablespoon each salt and pepper

  Place cleaned oyster shells, 1 ½ pounds of diced celery, 3 pounds of diced onions, bay leaves, thyme, and reserved corn cobs in a stock pot.
  Cover with water. Bring to a boil over medium-high heat, reduce heat to medium-low and simmer twenty minutes. Strain.
  In a large saucepan, fry bacon over medium-high heat. Drain off excess fat.
  Add the remaining celery and onions and sauté until almost fully cooked.
  Add the shucked corn and cream.
  Season with tarragon and reduce to ½ the original volume.
  Add the oysters and stock, a bit at a time, until you reach your desired consistency. Taste for seasoning, ladle into soup plates and garnish with tarragon sprigs.   (8 first course servings)

Recipe courtesy of Billy Birks, sous chef, Avalon, Eureka

As much as we love oysters, local residents await the Dungeness Crab season each year with eager anticipation. Jeff Sesar, who has cooked on both coasts, insists that Dungeness Crab is the best crab anywhere to work with. These crab cakes, made with generous chunks of Dungeness, are baked rather than fried. They're an exquisite alternative to those in the traditional style.

" Maryland" Crab Cakes
    5 whole eggs
    5 egg yolks
    1 cup mayonnaise
    3 pounds Dungeness crabmeat
    4 cups fresh croutons (cut from a crust-trimmed day-old baguette
        in ¾ inch cubes)
    juice of two lemons
    2 tablespoons Dijon mustard
    1 teaspoon chili powder
    1 teaspoon paprika
    1 tablespoon minced garlic
    1 cup diced yellow onion
    1 cup diced celery
    2 tablespoons chopped parsley
    4 tablespoons olive oil

Preheat oven to 400 degrees F.

In a bowl, whisk together the eggs, mayo, lemon juice, Dijon mustard, and herbs.

Add the crab meat and fresh croutons and mix well, trying not to break up the crab meat.

Heat 2 tablespoons oil in a sauté pan over medium-high heat.

Add onion, celery and garlic, and cook till vegetables are soft. Remove from heat and allow to come to room temp.

Form cakes on a non-stick sheet pan. Drizzle with olive oil to ensure browning. Bake ten minutes.

Lemon Aioli
    6 egg yolks
    1 ¼ cups extra virgin olive oil
    juice of 2 lemons
    1 teaspoon minced garlic
    1/8 teaspoon salt

In a mixing bowl, slowly drizzle oil into egg yolks, whisking vigorously.
Whisk in lemon juice, garlic and salt. Store cold.
For presentation, coat individual plates with aioli.
Top with crab cakes and serve immediately. (15 first course servings)

Recipe courtesy of Jeff Sesar, chef Moonstone Grill, Trinidad

A stainless steel pan is essential for making the champagne cream sauce. The champagne will react with any other metal causing the sauce to "break." The recipe is written as a first course, but it could easily be doubled to make four entrees.

Phyllo Purses of Crab with Champagne Cream Sauce

    12 ounces Dungeness Crab, picked over
    salt and pepper to taste
    ½ package phyllo dough
    2 ounces butter, melted

Preheat oven to 400 degrees F.

In a mixing bowl, season the crabmeat with salt and pepper.

Using three sheets of phyllo dough, stacked evenly on top of each other, cut the dough with scissors or a sharp paring knife into four-inch by four-inch squares. Brush the squares with melted butter.

Place one ounce (about one heaping tablespoonful) of seasoned crabmeat in the center of each three-layered square. Bring the corners of the pastry dough up to meet and press down just above the filling to form a purse shape.

Place purses on a baking sheet and bake ten to fifteen minutes, until golden brown.

Champagne Cream Sauce
>1 tablespoon butter
>1/4 cup shallots, finely chopped with a sharp knife
>pinch of salt
>1 cup champagne
>1 cup heavy cream
>seedless green grapes, halved, to garnish
>parsley, finely chopped, to garnish
>lemon zest, finely grated, to garnish

In a small stainless steel sauce pan, melt butter over medium-low heat. Add shallots and cook until tender, being   careful not to let them brown.

Add the champagne and a little of the salt. Increase the heat to high and bring to a boil to reduce the sauce to one third its original volume.

Add the heavy cream and cook, stirring often over medium-high heat until the sauce is smooth and thickened. Pass through a fine-mesh sieve to remove any bits of shallot.

Ladle cream sauce into each of four plates. Top with three of the purses. Garnish with grapes, parsley and lemon zest. (4 first course servings)

Recipe courtesy of Alex Begovic, Personal Caterer, Eureka

According to Chef Alex, the key to a real risotto is to make certain that every bit of onion is translucent, but none of it browns.

Crab Risotto

1 tablespoon butter
2 tablespoons olive oil
1 large white onion, finely diced
salt and pepper to taste
up to 8 cups of chicken stock
½ tablespoon tomato paste
2 cups Arborio rice
½ tablespoon ground garlic
3/4 cup dry white wine such as Chardonnay or Chablis
½ cup freshly grated Parmesan cheese
1 ½ pounds crabmeat, picked over to remove any bits of shell or cartilage
finely chopped fresh herbs of your choice for garnish
diced red bell pepper for garnish

In a large sauce pan over medium heat, melt the butter. Add olive oil and onion, and reduce the heat to low. Cook, stirring, until onions are completely translucent and tender, but not brown. Salt lightly.

Meanwhile, in another large sauce pan, combine chicken stock and tomato paste and bring to a simmer.

Turn the heat under the onions to medium and add the rice. Cook, stirring constantly, until the rice is almost completely translucent, about five minutes. Add the garlic and stir in the wine. Cook until the rice has completely absorbed the liquid. Start stirring in the chicken stock, one cup at a time, making certain that all the liquid is absorbed after each addition before adding more. Proceed in this manner until the rice is tender, but not mushy.

Turn off the heat. Stir in the Parmesan cheese and about ½ pound of the crabmeat. Season with salt and pepper, top with remaining 1 pound of crab, fresh herbs and diced red bell pepper. (6 servings)

Recipe courtesy of Chef Alex Begovic, Personal Caterer, Eureka

This is another of Alex Begovic's traditional French recipes. It is most often presented in scalloped shell-shaped dishes, but ramekins may be used instead. If you are able to use fresh scallops, be sure to clean both the scallops and their shells thoroughly. He recommends adding a small amount of salt at every step to make certain that the seasoning becomes thoroughly incorporated.

Sea Scallops au Gratin

For the sauce:
    salt and pepper to taste
    1 ½ tablespoons butter
    1/4 cup very finely chopped shallots
    ½ tablespoon ground garlic
    1 cup dry white wine such as Chardonnay or Chablis
    1 cup heavy cream
    4 large sea scallops

In a large stainless steel sauce pan, melt butter over medium heat. Add shallots and let cook until soft but not brown. Reduce heat if necessary.

Add garlic and cook briefly, one or two minutes.

Add wine and raise the heat to medium-high. Reduce sauce to one-third its original volume.

Add the cream and bring mixture to a simmer. Let it thicken for several minutes, but do not boil.

Drain the scallops thoroughly and season with salt and pepper. Season the sauce as well. Let sit, seasoned, for several minutes while you prepare the topping.

For the topping:

3 tablespoons melted butter
1 cup purchased bread crumbs
½ cup freshly grated (not shredded) Parmesan cheese
2 tablespoons minced fresh parsley
1 tablespoon chopped fresh thyme
½ tablespoon very finely grated lemon zest
salt and pepper to taste

Mix all ingredients thoroughly by hand. Set aside.

Turn on broiler.

Add scallops to the cream sauce and let cook two to three minutes until scallops become opaque or white.

Place four scallop dishes or oven- proof ramekins on a baking sheet. Ladle cream sauce into each dish, filling each dish about one-third full. Place a scallop in each dish.

Sprinkle each dish with crumb mixture.

Run under broiler until topping turns a rich, golden brown. Rotate pan, if needed, to ensure even browning.

Serve immediately.(4 entree servings)

Recipe courtesy of Chef Alex Begovic, Personal Caterer

Roosevelt Elk   © *Matthew Filar*

CHAPTER THREE

WILD THINGS

For lovers of the outdoors, much of the appeal of Humboldt County lies in its recreational opportunities. Eighty percent of the county's 2.3 million acres exists as forest lands, protected redwoods and recreation areas. The World Wildlife Fund has identified us as one of the most diverse ecosystems left on the planet.

The state of California has set aside seventy-five thousand acres here as state parks. The largest of these, Humboldt Redwoods, near the county's southern border, includes the thirty-two mile scenic highway known world-wide as the Avenue of the Giants. It also encompasses more than one hundred miles of biking, hiking and horse-back riding trails, and two hundred fifty campsites.

At the northern end of the county, Redwood National Park and Prairie Creek Redwoods State Park have been designated as a United Nations Biosphere Region and World Heritage site. Here, in addition to camping, biking, hiking and riding, visitors can enjoy a beautiful Pacific Ocean beach, large herds of Roosevelt elk, and a variety of ranger-led interpretive programs. Prairie Creek is also home to the not-to-be-missed Fern Canyon, a botanical wonderland where walls thirty feet high and completely covered by many species of ferns, rise from the canyon floor to a waterfall above.

The ocean and the county's six rivers afford a variety of water sports. Salt-water and fresh-water fishing, kayaking, white-water rafting, even whale watching draw visitors from around the globe. Camping, cycling, hiking, hunting, rock climbing, and rock hunting engage outdoor enthusiasts on land.

Each spring, bird watchers flock to Arcata to attend the annual Godwit Days shorebird celebration. The site of the festivities, the Arcata Marsh and Wildlife Sanctuary, not far from the heart of town, boasts over two hundred fifty different species of birds and mammals. On the Humboldt Big Day trip, birders consistently observe over one hundred species in a day, including the endangered Marbled Murrelet, Snowy Plover, and Spotted Owl.

Unusual wildlife has long been a factor in Humboldt County life. A Karuk tribal legend about "upslope persons" is viewed today as referring to early Big Foot sightings. The legend described these creatures as "hairy, large, strong, stupid and crude." They could also be deadly, and therefore were feared by the Karuks.

A Yurok legend, however, takes a very different view. It speaks of a young woman who vanished from her village. According to the tale, she ultimately returned with an infant, and baskets filled with precious dentalia shells, insisting that she had married a giant, one of a family of four who, she claimed, shouted from the hilltops.

In the twentieth century, a number of Big Foot sightings have been claimed in the area. Today, the town of Willow Creek celebrates Big Foot Days annually. In addition, the town's main drag, Highway 299, features a tiny Big Foot Museum and an enormous hand-carved redwood statue of the hairy beast, smack dab in the middle of town. Each year, the state department of Fish and Game issues hunting licenses for ducks, geese, grouse, pheasants, quails, wild turkeys, bear, cottontail rabbits, deer, and wild pigs. Hunters locally are passionate in their pursuits and many families here depend on game to keep their protein levels healthful.

Not all of Humboldt's wild treasures dwell in the animal kingdom, though. Foragers will boast at length about their findings and how cleverly they have used what they have found. Eric Hollenbeck, founder of the Blue Ox Millworks and Historic Park, is not boastful by nature, nor is he actually involved in food. Yet he is a true forager who has every right to be proud of what he has accomplished.

Over the years, Hollenbeck has discovered abandoned woodworking equipment in the forests. He has retrieved the machinery, restored it, and taught himself how it works. Today he recreates Victorian millwork on the original equipment. His pieces can be found at the White House and Camp David as well as in homes nationwide.

From little children with stained fingers and faces who pride themselves on buckets of wild berries, to hunters who feed their families on large and small game, to the folks who show up at restaurants and delight chefs with chanterelles and morels, county denizens thrive on wild things.

Just north of the tiny town of Orick, at the edge of Prairie Creek Redwoods State Park, Rolf's Park Café and Motel boasts the undisputedly best game menu around.

Rolf Rhineschmidt opened the restaurant in 1983 when his sons were seven and five years old respectively. Today, after training in their father's homeland of Germany, Stefan and Gerry have returned to Orick to assist him in the business. While the featured food is weighted with recipes from his background – his specialty, rahmschnitzel, is served at breakfast, lunch and dinner – it's the Game Combo that draws local people and out-of-towners to return again and again. Should you choose to eat outside under the redwoods, when the resident herd of Roosevelt elk wander into the neighboring meadow, you can watch 'em and eat 'em at the same time.

How did this award-winning continental chef end up in Orick? "That," he says, rolling his dark eyes, "is a long story." He tells it animatedly, in a deep, rich accent, punctuating the highlights with a nod of his white-maned head, a wry grin, or a graceful hand gesture.

He began his apprenticeship at the age of fourteen, and spent the next five years mastering every aspect of the hotel business. He plied his trade at various European sites before emigrating to Canada, then Florida, New York, and San Francisco. While he was on the West Coast, he took on the job as chef on the SS President Roosevelt. When his work aboard ship was done, he returned to Switzerland to open a restaurant. He discovered, that he had become too "American" to function in the rigid confines of a traditional European kitchen.

In 1972, he returned to northern California and became a partner in Santa Rosa's Black Forest Inn. While there, he and his family vacationed in Humboldt County and fell in love with all that it had to offer. When he came across a newspaper ad offering an Orick motel for sale, he bought it and converted a small gift shop on the property into a restaurant.

The size of the restaurant belies the length and the depth of the menu. The house breakfast special, for example, consists of a German farmer's omelet served family- style, with ham, bacon, sausage, mushrooms, cheese, potatoes and pasta. The whole is topped with sour cream and salsa, and accompanied by sourdough bread and preserves.

Lighter choices include a German apple pancake with whipped cream and strawberry-maple sauce, a bagel with a quarter pound of smoked salmon, cream cheese and fresh fruit, and a variety of egg dishes. Buffalo steak or elk steak in a wild mushroom sauce with eggs is a menu staple. And two people (or more) can share a German brunch of wiener schnitzel, rahmschnitzel, bratwurst, ham, and a farmer's omelet.

Lunch and dinner options, equally hearty and varied, feature many local foods: baked salmon, grilled red snapper, and depending upon availability, deviled oysters, crab ciaoppino, hasenpfeffer (hare), duck with wild rice, sautéed prawns and scallops in garlic sauce, even frogs' legs.

The rahmschnitzel, a fillet of pork with cream, wine and mushroom sauce, topped with Black Forest ham and cheese, never leaves the menu. Neither does the Game Combo: elk, buffalo and boar steaks served with champagne sauerkraut, wild mushroom sauce, creamed horseradish and cranberries.

Dinner comes in three courses beginning with a smoked salmon mousse, including bread, garlic butter, salad, fresh vegetables, potatoes, pasta, and ending with dessert and a glass of port wine.

Rolf graciously attributes his success to the people who have supported him since he opened in 1983. "People," he says, "are the best part of this business." The restaurant's guest register, filled with rave reviews from guests who come from all over the globe, indicates that the feeling is mutual.

He uses no written recipes, maintaining modestly that "everyone knows how to cook." Fortunately, although home-grown cooks may lack Rolf's continental training, newcomers to the area are sometimes also able to offer continental ways with game.

Binkey is not one of them. He does not fall into any such exotic category. He has spent his entire life in Humboldt County, and currently inhabits an RV somewhere near Orick. Social Security Disability pay, a result of several heart attacks, forms his only source of income. But the slight-built, gray-haired man takes one day at a time and feels he gets the most out of every one of them.

"I put on my coffee in the morning, and open the door of my RV, and the deer and elk come right up and say, 'Good morning.'"

He spent his earliest years around the Hoopa Reservation. There he acquired skills that he now uses to survive. A forager and a fisherman, Binkey loves to cook, and he describes with pride the meals he prepares and shares with his girlfriend.

"Here's something I found by accident. I caught some green ling cod, but I was out of flour and out of bread crumbs, too. I did have some Ritz crackers, though; so I crumbled them up real fine and used them to bread the fish. It's really good like that. You should try it sometime."

He gets a kick out of people who visit the area from big cities. "They pull up in their SUV's, loaded with expensive equipment, and start fishing nearby. After a few hours they'll ask me, 'How come you've caught all those fish and we haven't caught anything? What are you using for bait?' I'll tell 'em, 'Sand dabs,' and they'll say, 'What's a sand dab?' So I'll take my shovel and clear away a shovelful of sand and grab a few sand dabs for 'em. Sometimes the ladies won't use 'em. They're scared the sand dabs'll bite 'em. I tell 'em, 'Maybe a little, but they don't hurt.'

"Sometimes I tell 'em I'm using mussels, and they'll say they're using mussels too. But their mussels are out of the shell. That's not natural. Fish are too smart to fall for that. I'll show 'em how to crack the shell a little so they can get the meat on their hook, then wrap the shell back around it. Fish love it. They'll bite on that."

Binkey, health conscious after his hospital experiences, makes sure he gets a balanced diet. He gathers gallons of berries of every available variety and shares the bounty with friends and neighbors in the area. He enjoys the responses his gifts evoke, especially from the elderly who are no longer able to do their own berrying.

"This year I took a bunch of blackberries to the lady at the Palm Café. She made me a big batch of berry jam. I've given away most of it to the bus drivers who give me rides. I went to school with all of 'em. They know I can't pay the bus fare, but they pick me up anyway, so I give 'em what I can.

"And I know where to find plenty of vegetables, too. I can show you spots where artichokes grow wild. They're as big as your fist. Bigger, even. And wild asparagus, too. Most people don't know asparagus can grow as tall as a tree if you don't harvest it. And wild mustard greens. They're my favorite.

"I use wild onions and wild garlic. And every year I plant garlic on land I know about that nobody uses. That way, I always have a supply.

"I make a really good dish with fern tips cooked in a little butter till they just open up. But you don't want to cut all the tips from one plant or it won't come back. You take a few from each one. Then you'll always have more. Moss roots, too. Moss roots can be delicious.

"Do you like tea? I like mint tea, but I add a little Scotch broom and a little licorice (Anise) to the mint. Otherwise, it can get really strong. And I like to make tea from wild rose hips. It's a great source of vitamin C.

"My girlfriend is always really surprised at what I can cook for her. She says, 'God must have sent you to me.'" He lowers his eyes and brushes an imaginary speck from his spotless jeans, but his smile shows how much her praise means to him.

"You know, I never know what the date is, or even what time it is or what day it is. I don't need to keep track of those things. My life doesn't depend on 'em at all. But I sure know how to eat really well. *That's* important."

Many of us who grew up in the fifties and sixties agree that eating really well is important. And when we finally get a break from the work-a-day world, that's one of our first considerations. Enter a place described by *Bed and Breakfast Guide* as "Set on a cliff above perhaps the most stunning stretch of coastline in California." The place is the Lost Whale Bed and Breakfast Inn, and the food there is prepared by Margaret Haegart, a five-star chef who stumbled onto Humboldt County and, like so many others, found a place to live her dream.

So, considering dreams, what constitutes the perfect getaway space? Imagine a four-acre clearing in an ancient redwood forest, quiet except for the whispered rhythm of the ocean and the occasional barking of sea lions. Circle the perimeter with the lavish gardens broken only by a trail to a private beach. In the center of the clearing, plant a generous patch of meticulously manicured lawn, topped by a handsome inn.

Inside the building, let each room project a sense of serenity cloaked in style. Soften the decor with just enough frills to suggest personality and comfort. Outside, mount a broad deck with a hot tub. And for the *piece de resistance,* put a world-class chef in the kitchen.

It's no wonder the guest book records high praise:

- "a sense of rest and oneness with the earth"
- "I thought I'd lost my heart, but I believe I've found it again"
- "If there's a heaven, this is it."

Located five miles north of Trinidad, and opened in 1989, The Lost Whale has also garnered accolades from the press. The *San Francisco Chronicle* named it "One of the ten best dream vacation spots in California." And *American Historic Inns'* newsletter listed it as "One of the ten most romantic inns in the entire United States."

In 2003, Gary Haegart was approached by the owners and asked to manage the inn for a month. Haegert and his partner intended to build a bed and breakfast in Brookings, Oregon, and he thought that running The Lost Whale would be valuable experience. As one month stretched into many, he settled in. When the opportunity arose to make the arrangement permanent, he decided to go for it.

Haegart had an ace up his sleeve. His sister Margaret happens to be a phenomenal chef. Her career spans decades of experience around the world. She has opened many five-star restaurants including one at the Fontainebleau Hotel in Miami Beach, and five at Hilton Hotels. She's also served as personal chef to celebrities Frank Sinatra and George Burns, and has cooked underway for yacht owners as well.

At her brother's invitation, she arrived at The Lost Whale and took over as resident chef. Their devotion to each other becomes apparent in the easy banter between them. A clown by trade, Gary exudes a ready natural humor, and Margaret laughs heartily at his frequent quips. He, in turn, sings her praises as a chef and admires the passion she brings to her work. "She lives," he says, "to see the pleasure on people's faces when they eat what she's cooked."

He admits that he finds similar joy watching their guests unwind. "Many of them come in from high-stress jobs and big city living. You can see the tension in their faces when they arrive. Then they soak in the hot tub. They stroll through the gardens. They wander down to the beach. And after a while, the cloud lifts. They're smiling and holding hands.... It's like they're completely different people."

Down the road, just south of Trinidad, Chef Jeff Sesar presides over the Moonstone Grill. Sesar admits that he's had some great breaks in life. At fifteen years old, instead of bagging groceries or pumping gas, he went to work as a prep cook. His first big break came two years later when he apprenticed to a French chef in New Jersey.

"The first two years of my apprenticeship were spent in a small bistro with an even smaller kitchen where I got hands-on experience in every area. The next two years were in a large hotel where the kitchen had stations for each step. So I got immersed in two distinctly different experiences.

"When I was twenty-one, friends who had moved to Arcata urged me to come out and join them. When my apprenticeship was up, I decided to take them up on it. In 1987, I took over the kitchen at the Paradise Ridge Café. I was able to write menus, to find out about people's tastes. When that folded, people told me, 'Jeff, you're a chef. You really need to be in the Wine Country.' So I went down to Sonoma County and worked for a while at the Madrona Manor in Healdsburg." While there, he began to feel a need for further education. "I just felt like I wanted to solidify my knowledge in some areas." So he headed back to New York where he worked, went to school, and generally enjoyed city living.

Meanwhile, back in Arcata, Curley Tait was preparing to open Curley's Grill in Ferndale (see chapter five). Curley had run the kitchen for Tuck and Company, and partners Chris Smith and Bill Chino needed to fill the vacancy with someone tested, competent and creative. Smith asked his niece, Diana Dick, if she could suggest anyone. Dick, a graduate of California Culinary Academy, had worked with Sesar at Madrona Manor, and she recommended him. Several lengthy phone calls later, Sesar returned.

The operation at Tuck and Company was actually three restaurants: The

Plaza Grill, a one hundred sixty seat restaurant upstairs at Jacoby Storehouse; Abruzzi, a fine-dining spot at street level; and Abruzzi Catering. Sesar spent three years there reorganizing and revitalizing the food service functions and breathing new life into the menus. He next moved to Seattle, but Tuck and Company wasn't done with him yet. While he was gone, Sam Merryman, owner of the popular Merryman's Restaurant at Moonstone Beach in Trinidad decided to retire. Not wanting to see his life's work fall apart, Merryman approached Smith and Chino with an offer to sell the dinner house. They called Sesar again with an irresistible opportunity. If he would take over the kitchen, they would give him a year to update the space according to his own specifications.

Sesar returned once more. It took a year to do all that he wanted. The Moonstone Grill opened a year later with the same spectacular view of the Pacific, but a completely renovated kitchen. With all new wiring, all new equipment, and all new staff, Sesar has created a menu that shows off the best that Humboldt County has to offer. "People ask me to describe my style, but for me, it's not about style. I search out the finest possible ingredients and prepare them in a way that I hope lets them speak for themselves.

"Our guests are just that: our guests. We want them to come in and spend a pleasant evening here. We're not a "fill 'em up and rush 'em out" kind of a place. It's important that their preferences be honored. That can be hard if you've got any kind of ego. You go to great lengths to prepare a menu that showcases food perfectly, and someone comes in and wants his lamb very well done, or asks for catsup with his steak. But he's a guest. It's his dinner, and he can have it anyway he wants it.

"We've put together a granita. If we get backed up and it looks like it'll take more than twelve minutes between courses, our guests get a Margarita glass of granita. It cleanses the palate, and it keeps them from filling up on bread. And they don't feel as if they've been abandoned.

"I would like for people to have a real understanding of what they get when they go out to eat. Perhaps they're paying twenty-four dollars for a rack of lamb they could have fixed at home for twelve dollars. But they're not just getting a piece of meat. They're getting my training and experience, my staff's full attention, a quiet space where they can enjoy their meal uninterrupted. Dining

out isn't just about eating. It's about an entire experience. At Moonstone Grill,
I want that experience to be one they'll savor and remember for a long time."

Nearby, Sandra Fredrickson knows how relaxing life in the area can be.
When she retired from her position teaching nursing in San Francisco, she
moved to Westhaven, a small community across the freeway from Trinidad.
Her forested homestead far exceeded her expectations, with its comfortable
climate and a cultural environment above average. She only missed a social
circle in which to move.

To fill the void, she began spending Thursday mornings with a group of
women who put berry pies together. She's been doing it ever since.

Actually, she re-thinks, the truth is more complex and the process less
complex than it sounds. "Every Thursday" excludes time around major holidays
like Christmas. And, in fact, the pies are made every other Thursday. Jam- and
jelly-making fill in the alternate weeks. But, bottom line, many Thursdays each
year, she shows up at the Westhaven Fire Hall to help her new friends prepare
for the annual Westhaven Wild Blackberry Festival, held "always the last
weekend in July."

The festival debuted in 1960 as a way for the Westhaven Ladies Club to
raise funds for the community's Volunteer Fire Department. Initially, members
made pies at home, each from her own favorite recipe. About two hundred pies
showed up the first year, but the product lacked uniformity and quality control.
Gradually, things changed. The Fire Hall now serves as home to a huge walk-
in freezer able to store ready-to-bake pies, and an assembly line process and
standard procedures guarantee even quality in the finished product. In 2003,
over five hundred pies, plus nearly one thousand jars of jams and jellies, reaped
a net profit of seven thousand dollars.

The fund raising effort attracted the talent of Hans Giovanoli, former owner
of the Cherry Blossom Bakery in Eureka. Now retired from the business world,
he spends every other Thursday hand-mixing pie crust dough for the Westhaven
ladies. They say he also yodels for them on request. Each time, he makes two
large vats of dough, adding powdered milk to the mix to ensure the bottom
crusts brown evenly.

Once the dough is mixed, four ladies tackle the task of rolling it out to fill waiting pie tins. The crust-filled tins then move to "fillers" who scoop in premixed filling and add top crusts. Two "crimpers" finish the pies, marking each one to indicate whether the filling is wild blackberry, marionberry, or a combination. Finally, individually encased in Ziploc freezer bags, the pies rest on shelves in the Fire Hall freezer, awaiting the next festival where eager patrons snap them up whole, or by the slice.

Over the decades, the pie-making team has expanded to include volunteers from the McKinleyville Senior Center, and the proceeds now benefit more than just the volunteer firemen. The library, Rotary Club, Senior Center, and a scholarship fund each receive a portion of the profits. Other foods, beverages, crafts, games, and live music fill out an expanding venue, and a good time is had by all.

But for the ladies who work together all year, like Sandra Fredrickson, the rewards reach far beyond profits. She's made new friends to last a lifetime, and her retirement is now all she dreamed it would be.

In August, 2001, local aficionados came together and formed the Humboldt Bay Mycological Society. They aimed to further the knowledge of members and the general public regarding fungi in general and locally foraged fungi in particular. The group meets monthly, from September to May, to share and identify their finds, and to hear lectures from experts on topics ranging from the basic (Mushrooms 101) to the esoteric (Entolomatoid Fungi and Their Macroscopic Features).

Regularly scheduled guided weekend forays give members and non-members alike an opportunity to experience foraging first-hand. *The Mycolog,* their newsletter, issued during "mushroom months," keeps members updated on events and topics of specific interest.

Each November, when rain moistens the forest floor and fungi begin to form, the group hosts its annual Mushroom Fair. For several days before the event, foragers haunt their favorite sites gathering a broad spectrum of specimens along riverbanks, beneath redwood canopies, and from backyards. The haul varies, depending primarily on the weather, but HBMS members, a dedicated bunch, usually manage to secure several hundred different varieties to display and discuss with the hundreds of people who attend.

The day before the fair, volunteers gather at Redwood Acres Fairgrounds in Eureka to prepare Walter Vickers Hall for the celebration. They wrap tabletops with protective black plastic, knock together wooden boxes, and fill the boxes with forest findings. Duff (the material of forest floors), fern fronds, and other flora transform the containers into micro-environments which, in turn, cradle the foragers' prizes.

Long-time visitors begin to arrive the next day, a mind-boggling array awaits them. Posters detailing the interaction of trees and mushrooms, the medicinal properties of mushrooms, mushrooms in folklore and fairy tales, and guides to identifying mushrooms adorn the walls.

At one end of the room, an expert, equipped with several reference books, offers to identify visitors' finds and answer questions. At the other end, an open kitchen shows off a local chef preparing wild mushroom recipes, with the opportunity to sample finished products.

Along a long wall, edible species and toxic species afford close inspection. The fourth wall features field guides, cookbooks, tee-shirts, posters, and gifts decorated with mushroom motifs for sale. Membership information and enrollment forms are there as well.

In one corner, mushroom dyes, illustrated on skeins of fiber, demonstrate a lesser known aspect of the forest marvels. A vendor takes over another corner with kits of portabellas, creminis, white buttons, elm oysters and dense white mushrooms for those who want to try growing their own.

But the largest draw by far is the rectangular formation of tables in the center of the room, a veritable groaning-board of local fungi, remarkable for the diversity of size, color, texture and form. Large *Lycophyllum decastes, Boletus rubripes,* and *Cortiniarus ponderosus* contrast with tiny *Mycena rosella, Mycena strobilinoides,* and *Mycena rerida..* There are blood-red *Russala sanguinea,* burgundy-colored *Ganoderma oregonense,* and slate-blue *Albatrellus flettii.* High-domed, deep orange *Amanita muscaria* flecked with ivory-tinted spores looks like it was lifted from an illustration in a children's book. Golden orange *Dacrymyces palmatus,* gelatinous to the touch, appears more like crystallized resin that seeped from its tree-branch host than like the edible fungus it is.

From a nearly-black brown to stark white, with caps ranging from ruffled, to domed, to flat, to inverted, from glassy-smooth to "hairy," to seemingly chipped from coral reefs, the sheer numbers could overwhelm a neophyte. Fortunately, knowledgeable HBMS members stand by, ready to answer questions and help viewers absorb the scene.

Those who have yet to venture beyond the standard supermarket varieties may not realize that flavors vary widely as well. From the delicate oyster tree, to the intensely earthy porcini, to the smokey shiitake, there's a mushroom to compliment any savory dish. Sophisticated palates even detect specific accents reminiscent of almond, seafood or garlic in some of the lesser-known edible kinds. And HBMS holds annual potluck dinners so that members may further explore subtle flavor distinctions.

An earlier generation of American youth voiced as its popular put-down, "There's a fungus among us". For HBMS members, it's a celebratory boast.

NORTH COAST WAYS WITH WILD THINGS

While this recipe is typically French fare, it's a great way to prepare the wild pigs hunted here in California. Alex remembers it fondly from childhood when his grandfather brought home a boar he bagged.

Braised Boar with Chestnuts
    4 - 5 pounds of boar stew meat, cubed
    2 cups baby pearl onions (red, white or a combination)
    4 cups dry red wine (preferably Burgundy)
    1 cup dried cherries
    1 tablespoon juniper berries, crushed
    1 large bay leaf
    ½ tablespoon salt
    ½ teaspoon black pepper
    1 cup flour
    1 tablespoon fresh thyme, finely chopped
    2 tablespoons fresh marjoram, finely chopped
    4 cups carrots, washed, peeled, and sliced into coins
    ½ cup crushed tomatoes
    8 cups chestnuts, cooked and peeled wild mushrooms (optional)

In a shallow dish, combine meat, onions, cherries, wine, juniper berries, bay leaf, salt and pepper. Cover, refrigerate and marinate up to 48 hours (24 hours, minimum).

When ready to prepare, set a strainer over a large bowl, and pour in the marinated mix. Let drain for a few minutes, then sort out the meat from the onions and cherries, and reserve the liquid.

Put butter and oil in a large brazing pan over medium heat. Add carrots and sauté until golden brown and tender, but not mushy (about thirty minutes).

Add the onions to the pan and let brown a few minutes.

Dredge the meat with flour. Add to the pan and brown, stirring often.

Add reserved liquid and herbs. Salt and pepper the stew to taste, and bring to a boil. Cover and let simmer two hours, or until the meat is tender. Time may vary depending on the cut of meat.

Add the crushed tomatoes, cherries, and chestnuts during the last half hour of the cooking process. If using wild mushrooms, they may be added at this point as well, to give the meal an especially rustic flavor.

(8 very generous portions)

Recipe courtesy Chef Alex Begovic, Personal Caterer, Eureka

This preparation is consistent with the elegance guests have learned to expect from meals at 301. The recipe is included in The Carter House Cookbook, published by Ten Speed Press, along with a number of other delicious offerings by the Carters.

Marinated Grilled Rabbit in Basil Cream Sauce
   3 to 4 cups of white wine
   6 cloves garlic, crushed
   1 cup Tamari
   1/4 cup extra virgin olive oil
   1 tablespoon brown sugar
   liberal amount of rosemary, uncut
   fresh rabbit, cleaned and cut
   2 tablespoons scallions, finely chopped (white part only)
   1 tablespoon fresh lemon juice
   5 tablespoons water
   salt and pepper to taste
   1 cup fresh butter
   1 cup heavy cream
   1 cup fresh basil leaves
   squash blossoms, thoroughly washed
   fresh zucchini
   additional extra virgin olive oil

   Mix white wine, garlic, Tamari, 1/4 cup olive oil, brown sugar, and rosemary together. Marinate the rabbit in this mixture for six to twenty-four hours, turning occasionally. Save the marinade.
   Preheat the oven to 350 degrees F.
   In a roasting pan, pre-cook the rabbit for thirty minutes, basting occasionally with the reserved marinade.
   Heat the grill and cook the rabbit until done, about four minutes per side. Baste frequently with the marinade.
   Place scallions, lemon juice and water in a small saucepan over medium

heat. Add salt and pepper to taste and reduce until only about two teaspoons of the liquid remain.

In the top part of a double boiler, over simmering water, melt the butter. When it is liquefied, strain in reduced liquid from the sauté pan.

Slowly stir in the cream until the sauce is hot and completely blended. Season with salt and pepper.

Place basil in a food processor and puree thoroughly. Add the cream sauce to the food processor and blend well. Strain the resulting mixture.

Toss the squash blossoms in olive oil, salt and pepper. Place the blossoms in a hot oven just until they wilt.

Cut the zucchini into 1/4" to 1/8" julienne strips. Sauté the strips in olive oil and season to taste with salt and pepper.

To serve, cover the bottom of the plate with Basil Cream Sauce. Place rabbit on top of the sauce and surround with zucchini and squash blossoms.

(4 servings)

Recipe courtesy of Mark Carter, Restaurant 301, Eureka and Ten Speed Press

Chef Paul Clarke suggests that the sausage be prepared a day ahead of serving. Otherwise, omit the cheesecloth, wrap in buttered foil, and roast in the oven to the same internal temperature - one hundred fifty-five degrees Fahrenheit. A meat thermometer is essential.

App - Fresh Duck Sausage - with Dried Cherries and Jicama Slaw

½ pound pork butt, cubed
1 pound duck meat, cubed
1 teaspoon salt
½ pinch black pepper
pinch ground ginger
pinch allspice
1/4 cup ice water
1 whole duck skin, trimmed square
4 to 5 slices prosciuto
chicken stock for poaching
2 jicamas, shredded
1 red onion, sliced thin
2 carrots, shredded
1 cup mayonnaise
1 cup sour cream
1 ounce cider vinegar
1 ounce mustard
1/4 cup sugar
1/8 cup horseradish
1 cup dried cherries
1 cup additional chicken stock
½ cup red wine (Merlot, Pinot Noir, or Beaujolais)
salt, pepper, and sugar to taste
½ cup butter, cut in small pieces

Using a meat grinder, grind pork and duck through a 3/8 plate. Add salt, pepper, ginger and ice water. Mix well. Chill for at least one hour.

Wrap ground mixture in duck skin, prosciuto and cheesecloth. Twist one end and tie with butcher's twine. Twist other end to tighten, making certain to keep cheesecloth out of the roll. Tie off with more twine. Refrigerate.

When ready to prepare, poach in stock until well cooked, 155 degrees F in center, about forty minutes. Allow to cool in stock before slicing. Reserve one cup of the poaching liquid.

Grill the slices, or serve cold.

Mix jicama, red onion, carrots, mayonnaise, sour cream, vinegar, mustard, sugar, horseradish, salt and pepper. Chill one hour before serving.

Use reserved poaching liquid. Heat with cherries and red wine. Reduce by half, and finish with butter.

Season to taste and serve. (4-6 servings)

Recipe courtesy of Chef Paul Clarke, The Groves at Riverbend, Myers Flat

When Margaret serves this for breakfast at The Lost Whale Inn, you can hear the guests "Ooh" and "Ahh" and see them go back for seconds.

Lost Whale Blackberry Cobbler

4 cups blackberries, drained
1 ½ cups firmly packed brown sugar
2 tablespoons melted butter
1 ½ cups cake flour
1 egg
1 cup milled sugar
1 teaspoon vanilla extract
¼ teaspoon cinnamon
1 teaspoon baking powder
¼ cup vegetable oil
¼ cup half and half

Preheat oven to 350 degrees F.

Grease a nine-inch round pan with two-inch high sides.

Pour berries into prepared pan. Press brown sugar into berries and drizzle with melted butter.

In a large bowl, blend remaining ingredients. Pour over berry mixture. Bake for fifty-five minutes, then raise heat to 450 degrees and bake five minutes more, till golden brown. (8 generous servings)

Recipe courtesy of Margaret Haegart, Chef, The Lost Whale Inn, Trinidad

This is good at breakfast over pancakes, waffles or French toast. It's equally good on ice cream after lunch or dinner. For something really different, try it as a glaze for salmon, or lightly drizzled over goat cheese.

Blackberry Syrup

    5 cups blackberries, rinsed and drained
    1 cup sugar
    ½ cup water
    1 tablespoon fresh lemon juice

In a heavy three-quart saucepan over medium-high heat, blend all ingredients and bring them to a boil. Stir continuously until the sugar thoroughly dissolves. Lower the heat and simmer, stirring, about thirty minutes, or until the berries are very soft.

Place a fine sieve over a bowl, and slowly pour syrup into it, pressing to get the most syrup.

Refrigerate the syrup. Bring to room temperature before serving.

(1 ½ cups)

Use your favorite 2-crust pie crust recipe, purchase your pie crusts, or use Larry Martin's recipe found in chapter five (Farmers Market).

Bountiful Blackberries Pie

    pastry for a two-crust nine-inch pie

    4 cups fully ripe, freshly picked blackberries or Marionberries.

    1 cup sugar, plus 1 tablespoon

    1/3 cup sifted all-purpose flour

    1 tablespoon freshly squeezed lemon juice

    2 tablespoons butter, thoroughly chilled

    Preheat oven to 425 degrees F.

    Line nine-inch pie pan with pastry.

    Gently combine berries, 1 cup sugar, flour, and lemon juice. Pour into crust.

    Cut butter into small cubes (approximately 1/4 inch square) and sprinkle evenly over filling.

    Place second crust over all. Thoroughly seal edges, and slit top crust to vent.

    Sprinkle remaining tablespoon of sugar over top crust.

    Bake in center of oven until crust is golden-brown, about forty-five to fifty minutes.

    (8 servings)

Traditionally, "rillette" refers to a meat cooked in seasoned fat, then beaten into a paste and stored, covered with a layer of additional fat. This is a vegetarian version that goes quite well with good goat cheese.

Mushroom Rillettes

6 ounces butter, divided
½ pound assorted wild mushrooms, finely diced
1 shallot, minced
1 clove garlic, minced
½ cup mushroom stock (chicken stock may be substituted)
½ teaspoon fresh thyme, minced
½ teaspoon fresh parsley, minced
1/4 teaspoon fresh chives, minced
salt and pepper to taste
1 dash grated nutmeg

In a sauté pan over medium heat, melt four ounces of the butter. Add mushrooms, shallot, and garlic and sauté until dry.

Add the remaining butter, stock and herbs. Simmer until vegetables are tender.

Add the nutmeg and beat forcefully two minutes.

Cool in the refrigerator up to twenty-four hours. Bring to room temperature before serving.

(4 servings)

Recipe courtesy of Chef Matt Szymanski

This gravy can be made from any mushrooms, but Heather recommends using wild mushrooms - chanterelles, morels, oysters, or a combination of these. While this recipe meets vegan requirements, don't let that deter you. It will please everyone who enjoys mushrooms.

Mushroom Gravy (Vegan)
>   6-10 mushrooms, chopped
>   1 medium onion, chopped
>   1 tablespoon olive oil
>   2 ½ tablespoons soy sauce
>   ½ teaspoon cayenne pepper
>   1 teaspoon cumin
>   1 teaspoon savory (thyme may be substituted)
>   2 teaspoons black pepper
>   ½ cup flour
>   1 1/3 cup vegetable stock
>   1 teaspoon miso

In a medium-sized sauté pan over medium heat, sauté the mushrooms and onions in olive oil until the mushrooms are soft. Add soy sauce and spices and stir two minutes.

Add the flour and stir until vegetables are completely covered and the flour is lightly browned, three to five minutes.

Add the stock. Reduce heat to low and cook ten minutes. Remove from heat.

If gravy appears too thick, add water and stir in miso. If gravy is the desired consistency, add only the miso.

Recipe courtesy of Heather Maddox, Hurricane Kate's, Old Town Eureka

Curley serves this marvelous mélange stacked atop a grilled triangle of polenta made with vegetables, herbs and ricotta cheese.

Curley's Grill Portabella Mushroom Tower
 1 large portabella mushroom cap, sliced cross-wise
     in thirds (1/4 inch thick), divided
 2 slices eggplant, 1/4 inch thick, grilled
 3 slices zucchini, 1/4 inch thick, grilled
 2 slices summer squash, 1/4 inch thick, grilled
 2 slices tomato, 1/4 inch thick
 2 slices mozzarella, divided
 ½ ounce crumbled gorgonzola
 2 teaspoons olive oil

 Preheat oven to 450 degrees F.
 Stack the slices as follows: mushroom, eggplant, 1 slice mozzarella, mushroom, zucchini, summer squash, tomato, gorgonzola.
 Place tower on baking tray. Drizzle with olive oil, and bake five minutes.
 Remove from oven, add last mushroom slice and remaining mozzarella. Return to oven and bake for two minutes more.
 Place on a grilled triangle of polenta and serve immediately. (1 serving)

Recipe courtesy of Curley Tait, Curley's Grill, Ferndale

Produce Stand, Arcata Farmers Mkt. © *Matthew Filar*

CHAPTER FOUR

FARMERS MARKETS

"Fresh."

The word comes up repeatedly in conversations with local chefs and restaurateurs. It sets Humboldt County's dining options apart, ensuring peak flavors, eye-appealing presentations and maximum nutritional properties in everyday meals and special events.

The value of freshness can be seen, from April through November, in the enthusiasm of the crowds at the weekly Farmers Markets held around the county. Eureka's Old Town and Henderson Center neighborhoods, McKinleyville's Shopping Center and Wildberries Market in Arcata each host a three hour market on either Tuesday or Thursday. There, professional food workers and homemakers alike can select just-picked produce, freshly cut flowers or growing plants to add to their own gardens.

But the North Coast Growers' Association outdoes itself on Saturdays at the Arcata Plaza. Starting at 9:00 A.M., as many as two thousand shoppers descend on the square, some carrying baskets in which to haul their purchases home. They make their way around the plaza, checking out the latest harvest, chatting with vendors, sampling the offerings and bumping into old friends. In the center of it all, musicians take to a temporary stage to add a festive rhythmic backbeat to the scene.

In odd spots, you can watch jugglers perfect their skills. The vendors, elbow to elbow, surround the plaza with tables sagging under the weight of their merchandise. Brightly colored umbrellas compete with nature's own spectrum, visible in lug boxes of produce, buckets of blooms and pots of growing greenery. On one corner, The Angora Bunny Lady spins the fibers with which she creates the hats, scarves, socks and gloves she sells there. On another corner, the Growers' Association sells tote bags, posters and T-shirts all emblazoned with the season's logo, and disseminates information including directories to the one hundred or so member-growers.

Since the Market's inception in 1978, residents have eagerly followed the county's growing seasons, from peaches and cherries in the spring to corn and pumpkins in the fall. Strawberries, blueberries, blackberries and raspberries; heirloom tomatoes and Japanese eggplant; hot peppers and sweet peppers; white, gold, red and purple potatoes; everything from artichokes to zucchini shows up on the plaza.

Recently, the Arcata Main Street organization added a weekly Chefs of Bounty series. In the vintage 1857 Jacoby storehouse, across Eighth Street from the plaza, a guest chef, caterer or food producer demonstrates new, taste-tempting ways to enjoy the Market's offerings. The presentations include recipes and tastes, gratefully received by Market-goers who have developed a keen appreciation for the abundance surrounding them and a real handle on the concept of "fresh."

With vendors like North Coast Shellfish and Capricious Cheese, you can design an entire meal. Herb growers carry seasonings and tea blends. You can even pick up honey   to sweeten your tea, beeswax candles to light your dining room, and a bouquet to grace your table. And the one-on-one contact with growers adds a personal touch. It's the next best thing to growing your own – perhaps it's even better.

Touring the plaza on any Saturday, at first glance you might not think Stacey Kett looks anything like a farmer. This willowy young woman, with her long hair braided into numerous plaits tucked under the rim of her crocheted hat, more closely resembles a turn-of-the-twentieth-century governess. In truth, she spends long, hard hours working the soil, having been involved in farming since 1984.

"After a while, I realized I was spending most of my free time in the herb gardens," she explains in a soft voice. " I became interested in the medicinal properties of herbs and started taking classes. We took a field trip to southern Oregon where we toured large herb farms. I was like, 'Wow! People farm herbs, too!'"

Ultimately, Tap Roots came into being. Like most Farmers Market participants, Stacey's space is certified organic. She combines Bio-dynamics,

Permaculture and Sustainable Agricultural methods to grow the herbs she markets as roots, leaves, flowers or whole plants.

Her booth features bright bundles of bachelor's buttons, calendulas and lavender – or any other crops currently in bloom. A "bulletin board" display holds various packaged dried blossoms and leaves of culinary or medicinal herbs. In one corner, seedlings in small pots tempt do-it-yourself gardeners, and herbal honeys offer yet another way to access the medicinal properties of the herbs.

At the farm, on a non-Market day, her deft hands pluck blossoms from sweet clover, a current favorite. "I fall in love with each plant as I work with it. Right now, it's sweet clover and nettles. But before long, I'll be ready for something else, and something else will be ready for me. It's an ever-growing, ever-changing process."

She loves what she does, especially the freedom it offers in regard to scheduling her time. And she enjoys the sense of self-discipline she realizes from making it work. The economics, not surprisingly, present a challenge any farmer can identify with, but Kett values her spirit and consciously brings herself back to optimism when the going gets tough.

At another Market booth, David Reed retails the honey produced by Reed's Bees. Like many young men in the county, when he finished high school, he went to work in the timber mills. And, like many in his generation, he experienced the frustration and economic setbacks involved when that industry declined.

But Reed had an ace in the hole. His father had been a bee-keeper, and Reed had absorbed the skills of an apiarist in boyhood. Today he successfully runs up to three hundred hives spread over the greater part of the county.

It's a one-man operation. Reed does it all from what bee-keepers refer to as "robbing the hives" to packaging the finished product. His bees produce honey from both wild flowers and blackberry blossoms, honey he sells himself at the Farmers Market and at local food stores. In addition to pure honey and honeycomb, he now carries a variety of beeswax candles and a whipped honey blended with crushed raspberries that customers line up to sample.

Natural food fans have long touted the benefits of consuming honey. It contains small amounts of various B vitamins, 2.2 milligrams per hundred milligrams of vitamin C, and minerals including calcium, iodine, iron and magnesium. Its advocates claim its efficacy in treating digestive disturbances, upper respiratory ailments and various eye disorders. Honey has also been used for centuries to treat skin problems. "During the Civil War," Reed says, "they applied honey to the bandages used on wounds. It's a natural antibiotic."

What about the idea that beekeepers don't get arthritis? "That's a pretty broad statement," he admits. "But bee stings do stimulate the natural production of cortisone in the body, and bee-keepers probably have a lower incidence of arthritis than the general population. I recently read about people keeping bees with the deliberate intention of getting stung in order to alleviate the symptoms of certain debilitating conditions."

But watching Reed serve his customers at the Farmers Market on Saturdays, one gets the sense that honey is just plain good – good and gooey. He moves back and forth along the breadth of his display, dipping small plastic spoons into various containers and passing the spoons into outstretched hands, following up quickly with paper towels and laughter as the sticky sweetness escapes the confines of the mini-utensils. All the while, he greets familiar faces, takes money, makes change, bags products, answers questions, restocks emptying spaces, and plugs in all the other gaps that crop up for an entrepreneur in a one-man business. It's a grand ballet with Reed performing every step.

He expresses frank appreciation for having a reason to get up every morning, and for plenty to do during the day. Having experienced joblessness, he also values the revenue-producing aspect of what he does. But Saturday mornings on the Plaza, when the bands play and the crowds gather, David Reed makes it look like fun.

If you're in the market for fresh blueberries, you can stop by the booth staffed by the people from Wolfsen Farms. Or you can travel a winding country road in northeast McKinleyville from the end of June to early August, to the farmstead. There, you can take up a brightly colored plastic bucket and head out into the fields to pick your own.

Herb and Elaine Wolfsen originally grew conifer and redwood seedlings for the United States government on their ten-acre farm. But when a co-worker of Elaine's moved to Oregon to raise blueberries, the Wolfsens drove up to check out the operation, liked what they saw, and bought seven thousand plants to put in at home.

"Everybody told me 'You can't grow blueberries in Humboldt County,' and I thought, 'Oh, no. What have I done now?' But you can see they were wrong." He extends his arm to indicate the fifteen thousand thriving blueberry plants which now constitute the farm's sole crop.

Blueberry growers everywhere know that birds pose an enormous threat to a successful harvest. "In Oregon, they use a chemical that makes the birds sick. We don't do that here, though. We're certified organic," he says with pride.

Instead, the Wolfsens employ six-foot nets to protect the berries from feathered predators. "They work pretty well," Wolfsen says. "Of course, when we're working around the plants or harvesting the berries, we have to uncover them, and a few birds will sneak in. But generally, the nets are effective."

The organic certification offers an extra advantage to the crowd the Wolfsens call the "you-picks." It allows them to sample the seven different varieties grown on the farm right in the fields. That way they can decide which ones they prefer before they fill their buckets. Wolfsen encourages the sampling because each variety has its own flavor, and because pickers learn by sampling which berries are fully ripe and at their flavor peak.

"A few people take advantage," he says. "More berries end up in the picker than in the bucket. I can always tell which ones they are, because they'll watch me while they're eating. But overall, the sampling is a good idea."

Certainly the pickers enjoy it. Blueberry picking is not the stoop labor required by strawberries. And unlike the area's abundant blackberry vines, blueberries are thorn less. So Wolfsen Farms offers an ideal family outing on the county's mild summer days, and a means to stock the family freezer at bargain prices.

Initially, the Wolfsens marketed exclusively to northern California grocers featuring organic produce, and to the Saturday Farmers Market. But the word got out about locally-grown blueberries, and requests began to come in from people who wanted to enjoy the advantages of picking their own. Eventually, the local newspaper got wind of the trend and ran a full-page spread on the operation, and the "you-picks" showed up in droves.

"I used to make long-haul runs down to the San Francisco Bay area. Berkeley Bowl (a large organic produce center in the East Bay) bought everything I could bring them. This last season they were real disappointed that I couldn't provide as many berries, but I told them I couldn't help it. The 'you-picks' cleaned me out."

Wolfsen estimates that they sell in excess of thirty thousand pounds of blueberries each season. And seeing the appreciation of those who come to pick ranks high on his list of perks for doing what he does. "Face it," he says. "Farming is hard, dirty work. But people keep telling us how much they value our being here.

"I look at it," he continues, "like raising children. With children, when they're little, you've got the diapers, the late-night feedings, the messes they make, all the things that make raising children hard, dirty work. But the growth makes it worthwhile. Watching your children grow up healthy, strong and productive provides real satisfaction. Farming is like that. The growth offers the same kind of reward."

Potters Produce, another Farmers Market vendor, also offers patrons an opportunity to visit the site and pick their own produce and to find their way through a corn maze in the fall.

In 1975, Denis Potter left Savannah, Georgia, in search of a more accommodating climate. That move brought him to Humboldt County where he taught industrial technology at Humboldt State University. Three years later, he and his wife, Julie, added truck farming to their schedule. In those days, they grew forty-five varieties of produce, notably broccoli, cauliflower, beans, lettuce and squash. "At the peak of the season," he recalls, "We'd harvest up to two thousand pounds of zucchini in a week."

It made for a grueling schedule. "We'd start with seedlings in the greenhouses in March, and go right through November without a break. I'd get home in the afternoons and go to work in the fields. I spent weekends and holidays working. I made deliveries to markets and restaurants six days a week."

He sees it as adding a sense of realism to what he had to say in the classroom. "Whether you're designing a widget or growing a vegetable, there are still problems to solve and strategies to plan," he explains. "While I saw it in part as a diversion from teaching, in fact, I was utilizing many of the same principles I was explaining to students."

Putting those principles to use is still what he enjoys most, even though he has retired from teaching. "I like the problem-solving and the challenge of making the business work." To this end, the Potters have made some big changes in their operation.

"We now limit our growing to pumpkins and corn, with a few winter squash. Everything is ready to harvest at the same time, in October. Then we get to take a vacation." The concentration has had serendipitous consequences, however. In 2002, the Potters planted their first corn maze and opened it to the public toward the end of the growing season.

The pumpkin patch gets its share of public traffic as well. As Halloween approaches, bus loads of school children from as far north as Orick, and as far south as Rio Dell, descend on Potters Produce – up to three thousand a season. They're treated to an old-fashioned hay ride and go home with a pumpkin they've selected from the patch.

"We actually lose money on the kids," Potter admits, "but it's our way of giving something back to the community." Watching the young visitors romp in the haystack, seeing their pride as they struggle to carry their pumpkins back to the parking lot, it's easy to see that profit isn't the only payoff for a project like this.

"But," the former industrial technology professor maintains, "it *is* a business." And for the residents of Humboldt County, the Potters' business is a continuing source of pride and pleasure.

While visiting the Farmers Market, be sure to cross over to the Jacoby Storehouse. In the center of the first floor, a local chef will be preparing something delicious to demonstrate the versatility and quality of the Market's offerings. One such recent demonstration featured Alex Begovic who headed the catering arm of Abruzzi, an upscale Italian restaurant housed in the Storehouse building.

Begovic cooked his first omelet at the age of seven. "Everyone in my family cooks," he says. "My father owned a restaurant. My brother is a chef. My sister is a marvelous cook."

He grew up in the country outside Paris, France, an area he says resembles Monet's paintings. "My grandfather used to take me hunting," he recalls. "Actually, we did very little hunting. It was more like a nature walk in the woods with the dog. My grandfather taught me so much – not of French culture, really, but of closeness to the earth. I so often find myself thinking of the things I learned from him.

"I remember when he would bring a rabbit home for dinner, the way he touched it when he dressed it. And we would go out and gather chestnuts together. He showed me how to crack them the old way, with his feet. Then we would roast them in the fireplace and eat them – especially at Christmastime.

"We always ate a lot at Christmas. Have you ever heard of a Norwegian omelet? It's like a big cake. You cover it with a hard meringue. Then you cover that with a soft meringue. You *flambé* it with vodka, then they turn out all the lights in the dining room and you bring it in. It's spectacular. The fire makes the top all golden brown...." His voice trails off, just for a moment; his bright, brown eyes appear to focus on some distant scene, and then he's back, delivering rapid-fire information, in Gallic accent, on his history with food.

Begovic came to the United States in 1990, at the age of eighteen. Like many luminaries in local food service, he tested the waters in several other places before discovering Humboldt County. Beginning in New Jersey, he migrated to New York state, then to San Francisco where he did some catering and worked at Moose's Restaurant. From there, he moved to Seattle where he manned the kitchen at *Place Pigalle*, a popular spot at Pike's Place Market. Next, he became chef at Brother Boyd's Bistro, then executive chef at the lightning-paced California Catering in Renton, Washington.

But by then, the auburn-haired boy who had walked in the woods with his *grandpere* had children of his own, and he found himself longing for a more family-friendly setting in which to bring them up. The Eureka-Arcata area proved to be the perfect choice.

Recently, he opened his own catering business. While he will take on major events, he hopes that the bulk of his business will be preparing elegant dinners in private homes. As he has always done, he will work with each client to create exactly the experience they want.

He enjoys the special challenges catering involves, but in the back of his mind he nurtures the dream of a restaurant of his own. He admits that his style, which he describes as "neo-American fusion," has changed since he arrived here, although traditional French dishes still form the base from which he draws.

"Many people in this area are interested in organic foods," he reports. "And a lot of people – whole families, even little children – are vegetarian. I'd like to offer a really nice place where they have a lot of choices. There are so many good things you can do with food without using meat."

As a recent Chefs of Bounty presenter, Begovic prepared chevre-topped polenta squares garnished with pesto or kalamata olives. The slightly grainy firmness of the polenta formed an ideal foundation for the buttery smoothness of the goat cheese. The combination of flavors proved both savory and mildly piquant, and the overall appearance was elegantly reminiscent of petit-fours "frosted" by a visual artist. The child who cooked his first omelet in a French country kitchen has grown into a welcome addition to the food scene half a world away.

NORTH COAST WAYS WITH PRODUCE

This traditional French country recipe makes excellent use of the produce stalls at the Market. Even if you think you might not care for one or more of these vegetables, do yourself a favor and try the soup anyway. You may be surprised at the richness of flavors, tempered by roasting, and perfectly combined.

Cream of Roasted Root Vegetable Soup
    1 medium onion, peeled and quartered
    1 medium potato, peeled and quartered
    1 medium carrot, peeled and cut smaller than the potato
    1 1/4 tablespoon olive oil
    2 ½ tablespoons dry sherry
    salt and pepper to taste
    1 medium rutabaga, peeled and quartered
    1 medium turnip, peeled and quartered
    2 good-sized ribs of celery, cut in 2-inch pieces
    water to cover vegetables.
    1 cup heavy cream
    2 tablespoons finely chopped parsley for garnish

    Preheat oven to 350 degrees F
    Combine the onion, potato, and carrot in a bowl. Season with olive oil, sherry, salt and pepper. Lift vegetables from the bowl, allowing excess seasonings to drain back into the bowl. Spread the vegetables in a single layer in a shallow roasting pan and roast until they are fork tender, fifty to sixty minutes. Place in a soup pot.
    Repeat this procedure with rutabaga which will need to cook about an hour and a quarter to an hour and a half.
    Repeat the procedure again with the turnip. This will also need an hour and a quarter or more to roast to the desired doneness.
    Repeat with the celery, checking for doneness after twenty minutes.

When all vegetables are in the soup pot, add enough water to barely cover them. Bring the soup to a simmer over medium heat and cook long enough to thoroughly heat the vegetables through, five to ten minutes.

While soup simmers, place the cream in a small saucepan and bring it to a simmer over medium heat.

In a blender, puree the soup in batches and return to heat. Add the simmered cream, combine thoroughly, and taste for seasonings. Ladle the soup into bowls, garnish with finely chopped parsley, and serve at once.

(4 servings)

Recipe courtesy of Chef Alex Begovic, Personal Caterer, Eureka

In toasting the peanuts, keep them moving all the time. Over-toasting them will make them bitter. If you prefer, you may substitute two cups of peanut butter.

African Peanut Soup

    2 cups shelled raw, unsalted peanuts
    ½ cup sliced celery
    ½ cup peeled and sliced carrots
    1 cup diced onions
    olive oil to coat pan
    2 garlic cloves
    1 ½ teaspoon kosher salt
    freshly ground pepper
    1 tablespoon ground marjoram
    1 tablespoon dried thyme
    1 ½ cup broccoli florets
    3/4 cup cauliflower florets
    6 cups vegetable stock
    fresh herb sprigs for garnish

In a heavy skillet over medium heat, toast the peanuts, stirring continuously, until they are evenly golden brown. Pour into a stainless steel bowl and allow them to cool.

Pour olive oil into a heavy stock pot to a depth of 1/8 inch. Turn heat to medium-low. Add the celery, carrots and onions, cover and sweat until onions are translucent.

Add garlic, salt, pepper, marjoram, thyme, broccoli and cauliflower. Cover and cook until the broccoli becomes a rich green. Add the stock and raise heat to medium-high.

Grind the peanuts to the consistency of brown sugar. Ladle a little soup liquid into a small saucepan. Stir in the peanuts, mixing well, then add to the soup. Simmer twenty minutes. Serve garnished with fresh herb sprigs.

(6 servings)

Recipe courtesy of Marie Wilkins Owner-Chef, Bless My Soul Café, Eureka

In sharing this recipe, Mike Vitiello commends its creator: "I wouldn't have thought this would work, but it's great." The combination of sweet potatoes and spicy peppers dances on the tongue, tantalizing all the taste buds.

Spanish Sweet Potato and Pepper Soup

3 poblano chilies
2 jalapeno chilies
small amount of canola oil
2 tablespoons unsalted butter
2 medium white onions
1 tablespoon cumin
1 tablespoon dried oregano
1 tablespoon minced garlic
2 pounds sweet potatoes, peeled and chopped
1 quart vegetable broth
1 cup heavy cream
juice of 2 limes
pinch of salt
fresh cilantro sprigs to garnish

Preheat oven to 375 degrees F.

Brush chilies with canola oil, spread on a baking sheet, and roast, turning every fifteen minutes, until skin is blistered and dark, thirty to forty-five minutes. Remove from oven and place immediately in an airtight container for fifteen minutes to sweat off the skin. Remove from container, peel, remove seeds and chop.

Peel and dice the onions to 1/4-inch pieces. In a stockpot over medium heat, melt butter, add onion and sauté until translucent. Add cumin, oregano and garlic and sauté five minutes more.

Add the sweet potatoes, peppers and vegetable broth. Bring to a simmer and cook until the sweet potatoes are tender enough to crush with a fork.

Remove the soup from the heat. Puree, thoroughly, in small batches, passing each batch through a fine-mesh sieve. Place strained puree in a large saucepan over low heat.

When the soup begins to simmer, add the heavy cream , lime juice, and a pinch of salt.

Ladle into bowls and garnish with sprigs of fresh cilantro.

(4 servings)

Recipe by Chris Smiley, courtesy of Mike Vitiello, Hurricane Kate's, Eureka

Since this recipe is made to order, the amounts are for a single serving. You can multiply the ingredients by the number of people you're serving. It's guaranteed to please.

Curley's Grill Recipe for Salad Nicoise

For dressing:
   1 cup Balsamic vinegar
   ½ cup Dijon mustard
   salt and pepper to taste
   1 teaspoon dried oregano
   2 cups olive oil

Whisk vinegar, mustard, salt, pepper and oregano together. Continue whisking and slowly add the olive oil in a steady stream until emulsified.

For the salad:
   1 large bowl of romaine and spring greens, torn into bite-sized pieces
   2 ounces of the dressing (recipe above)
   1 red potato, boiled until tender and quartered
   4 green beans, trimmed and boiled until tender
   1 fresh tomato, cut into 4 wedges
   1 hard-cooked egg, peeled and quartered
   1 ounce capers
   8 Nicoise olives, pitted
   1 4-ounce portion grilled fish fillet
   1 lemon wedge

Toss Romaine and spring mix with dressing in a large, chilled salad bowl. Arrange potato, green beans, tomato, egg, capers and olives attractively on top. Place fillet, drizzle with dressing, and garnish with a twist of lemon. (1 serving)

Recipe courtesy of Curley Tait, Curley's Grill, Ferndale

Although any greens will work in this salad, Alex has made his choice to maximize the impact of color and texture.

Wilted Greens with Bacon, Croutons, and Raspberry Vinaigrette
½ cups chopped thick-sliced bacon
½ cup very finely chopped shallots
2 teaspoons ground garlic
½ cup raspberry vinegar
1 bunch ruby chard
1 bunch mustard greens
1 bunch kale
1 bunch spinach
fresh cracked black pepper
1 cup seasoned croutons

Wash all greens. Pat dry and tear into bite-sized pieces.

In a large sauté pan over medium-high heat, cook the bacon until lightly crispy. Drain out bacon fat and reserve. Reserve bacon bits separately.

Return pan to medium heat. Add shallots and let cook.

Meanwhile, set another large sauté pan over high.

Add garlic to first pan, stir in, then deglaze with the vinegar and remove from heat.

Add two tablespoons of bacon fat to the second pan and use to sauté the greens. When greens are wilted, season with pepper and pour shallot, garlic and vinegar mix over them. Serve immediately garnished with bacon and croutons.

(8 servings)

Recipe courtesy of Chef Alex Begovic, Personal Caterer, Eureka

In preparation for the salad dressing, Chef Paul Clarke roasts garlic cloves, completely covered in olive oil, at 400 degrees F. When they are lightly browned, he removes the garlic and strains the oil, then uses both in the dressing.

Artichoke Hearts Salad

4 artichokes
water
2 lemons
½ cup balsamic vinegar
2 tablespoons Dijon mustard
2 tablespoons roasted garlic, chopped
4 tablespoons honey
1/4 cup canola oil
1/4 cup roasted olive oil
2 teaspoons chopped oregano
2 teaspoons chopped thyme
salt and pepper to taste
1 head radicchio
1 head Bibb lettuce
1 cup lettuce chiffonade
1 cup basil chiffonade
1 12-ounce can hearts of palm
1 red onion, sliced
1 bunch parsley

Using a thick towel or wearing cut-proof gloves, trim any stalk and hard outer leaves from the artichokes with a sharp knife. Remove the choke with a small spoon. Store the artichoke hearts in water, acidulated with the juice of one lemon until needed.

Poach the artichoke hearts in just enough water to cover, the juice of one lemon, and a little salt until a knife can be inserted easily into the base – about twenty minutes.

Cool in the cooking water to prevent discoloration and dehydration, then refrigerate until needed.

Combine the vinegar, garlic, mustard and honey in a bowl and mix well. Add the oils very slowly, whipping continuously, only until the dressing is emulsified. Avoid over beating which will cause the dressing to break down.

Add the oregano, thyme, salt and pepper. Taste for seasonings, adjust as needed, and store the dressing, covered, in the refrigerator until serving.

Use the radicchio and Bib lettuce to form four cups. Add the lettuce chiffonade and basil chiffonade to the cups as a base.

Quarter the prepared artichoke hearts and arrange over the base.

Cut the hearts of palm in thin strips and arrange with the artichoke hearts.

Finish with sliced red onion and chopped parsley.

Dress lightly, and serve extra dressing at the table.

(4 servings)

Recipe courtesy of Chef Paul Clarke, The Groves at Riverbend, Myers Flat

If you can find amaretti bread crumbs, usually available in Italian or specialty food stores, by all means use them in this recipe. They make an amazing difference in the flavor of the final product.

Ravioli di Zucca

2 pounds winter squash (pumpkin, butternut, kabocha) halved,
    then cut in small wedges
salt water to add to pan
4 ounces Parmigiano Reggiano cheese, grated
2 small eggs
fresh grated pepper to taste
whole nutmeg to taste.
2 cups all purpose flour
4 egg yolks
1 ½ tablespoons olive oil
12 ounces butter
2 tablespoons fresh sage, cut in thin strips

Preheat oven to 350 degrees F.

Sprinkle the squash with a little salt. Place in a roasting pan, adding a little water, and bake until thoroughly cooked, slightly browned and dry, fifteen to twenty minutes. Peel and puree the squash and let it cool.

Combine cooled squash puree with bread crumbs, cheese, one small egg, salt, pepper and nutmeg. Mix well, taste for seasonings and adjust if needed. Set aside.

In a food processor combine flour, egg yolks, the remaining small egg, olive oil, and a touch of salt. Pulse until the dough starts to form into a ball. Turn out on a pastry board and knead for ten minutes. Wrap the dough in plastic and let it rest for thirty minutes.

In a small saucepan over medium-high heat, brown the butter. Reduce heat to low and stir in the sage. Keep warm until needed.

When dough has fully rested, roll it out until you can read a newspaper headline through it. Place little mounds, about one heaping tablespoon each, evenly spaced, across half the pasta. Fold remaining half over the filling, taking care to gently squeeze out any pockets of air. Using a fluted pastry wheel, cut the ravioli into individual pillows.

Fill a large saucepan with water and bring to a boil. Add ravioli, one at a time, keeping the boil. Cook three minutes, then drain. Serve dressed with browned butter and sage.

(6 servings)

Recipe courtesy of Chef Matt Szymanski

Billy Birks created this recipe expressly around Farmers Market products. It calls for a spicy lettuce mix he gets from the Little River Farm stall. If you can't find a similar mix, try experimenting to create your own.

Cypress Grove Chevre with Watercress and Baby Greens, White Balsamic Vinegar and Roasted Baby Vegetables

    1 large shallot
    1 teaspoon Dijon mustard
    ½ cup white balsamic vinegar
    1 ½ cups olive oil
    salt and pepper to taste
    1 bunch baby carrots
    1 bunch baby turnips
    1 bunch baby beets
    3 ounces olive oil
    2 heads garlic, halved
    1 bunch fresh thyme
    salt and pepper to taste
    12 ounces soft Cypress Grove chevre
    6 ounces toasted walnuts or 6 ounces toasted pecans, crushed
    3/4 pounds spicy lettuce mix
    ½ bunch chives, chopped
    salt and pepper to taste.

In a blender, chop the shallot thoroughly with the mustard and vinegar. Slowly add the olive oil until vinaigrette is able to coat the back of a spoon. Season to taste with salt and pepper and refrigerate until ready to use.

Clean each vegetable and remove the tops. Cut each vegetable in half, lengthwise, and reserve separately. Using one large sauté pan for each vegetable, heat one ounce of oil in each pan until just smoking. Divide the thyme and garlic evenly between the pans, followed immediately by the vegetables. Brown, but do not burn, the vegetables on each side. If they begin to get too dark, add an ounce of water to the pan to stop the browning. Season with salt and pepper and set aside separately.

Roll the cheese into two-ounce cylinders, and roll each cylinder in crushed toasted nuts.

Toss the lettuce with the vinaigrette and divide onto six plates. Top each salad with a nut-crusted cheese cylinder.

Arrange some of each baby vegetable on each plate.

Finish with a sprinkling of chopped chives.

(6 servings)

Recipe courtesy of Billy Birks, sous chef, Avalon, Old Town, Eureka

Mike Vitiello built the smoker he uses at Hurricane Kate's and offers the following guidance for creating your own: Use a perforated pan that will fit tightly into another solid metal pan. Place a small piece of wood, about one inch by eight inches, in the bottom of the solid pan. The bottom of the perforated pan should rest at least one inch above the wood so that the smoke can circulate freely and evenly. Lid your contraption and place it on a burner over high heat. As soon as you see smoke billowing out from under the lid, place the tomatillos inside the perforated pan in a single layer. Smoke for three to five minutes.

Southwestern Frittata with Smoked Tomatillo Sauce

1 pastilla pepper
1 red bell pepper
1 green bell pepper
½ bunch fresh cilantro
7-10 mushrooms
1 red onion
½ cup cotija cheese, finely cubed
1 cup white cheddar cheese, shredded
8 eggs
½ teaspoon white pepper
½ teaspoon black pepper
1 teaspoon salt
½ teaspoon ground cumin

Preheat oven to 350 degrees F.

Remove stems and seeds from the peppers.

Cut all vegetables into bite-sized pieces. Place in an eleven inch by one and one half inch tart pan with a removable bottom with half of the cotija and half the white cheddar. Whip eggs with the spices and pour over the vegetables. Bake fifteen minutes. Remove from oven, top with remaining cheese and return to the oven. Continue baking until the eggs are set, about fifteen more minutes.

Serve immediately with Smoked Tomatillo Sauce.

Smoked Tomatillo Sauce
  2 ½ pounds purple de Milpa tomatillos, smoked
  4 jalapenos, seeds removed, coarsely chopped
  1 red bell pepper, seeds removed, coarsely chopped
  ½ cup canned green chili
  2 cloves garlic, peeled
  1/4 teaspoon ground cumin
  ½ teaspoon white pepper
  ½ bunch cilantro
  ½ teaspoon salt

Place all ingredients into a medium pan and cook over a medium-low flame for thirty minutes. Let sauce cool.
  Pulse in a food processor.
  (8 servings)

Recipe courtesy of Mike Vitiello, Hurricane Kate's, Old Town Eureka

Chef Larry Martin says he always puts strips of foil around the edges of his pie crusts to keep them from getting too brown. He removes the foil for the last fifteen minutes of baking time.

Lou's Favorite Rhubarb Pie

  4 cups sliced fresh rhubarb
  4 cups boiling water
  1 ½ cups, plus 1 tablespoon, sugar
  3 tablespoons, plus 1 tablespoon, flour
  1 teaspoon quick-cooking tapioca
  1 egg
  2 teaspoons cold water
  2 tablespoons cold butter, diced to 1/4 inch
  small amounts of milk and sugar
  1 recipe Perfect Pie Crust

Preheat oven to 400 degrees F.

Place rhubarb in a colander and pour water over it. Set aside to drain.

In a bowl combine 1 ½ cups sugar, 3 tablespoons flour and the tapioca. Mix well. Add the rhubarb and toss to coat. Let stand fifteen minutes.

Beat together egg and water and add to the rhubarb, mixing well.

Line a nine-inch pie plate with bottom crust. With your fingers, spread 1 tablespoon sugar and 1 tablespoon flour over bottom crust, making sure to cover completely. This will keep the crust from becoming soggy. Add the filling, dot with the butter and cover with top crust, cutting off excess pastry and sealing the edges. Cut slits in the top, brush with a little milk and sprinkle with sugar.

Bake at 400 degrees F. for fifteen minutes. Reduce heat to 350 degrees and bake another forty to fifty minutes, until crust is browned and filling is bubbly.

Perfect Pie Crust

　　3 cups flour
　　1 1/4 cups butter-flavored Crisco
　　1 pinch salt
　　1 egg, slightly beaten
　　1 tablespoon cider vinegar
　　5 tablespoons cold water.

In a large bowl, cut shortening into flour and salt mixture until it resembles coarse meal.

Mix egg, cider vinegar and water thoroughly. Combine with dry ingredients, mix well and form into a ball. Wrap in plastic wrap and chill for twenty to thirty minutes.

Unwrap dough and roll out to 1/8-inch thick. Any surplus dough may be wrapped and frozen.

(1 double crust and 1 single crust)

Recipe courtesy of Chef Larry Martin, Gingerbread Mansion Inn, Ferndale

Mike Vitiello gets all his apples from Clendenon's orchard in Fortuna. For this dessert, he swears by their Waltana variety. He reminds us, too, to pile the apples on generously because they will shrink as they cook.

Apple Crumble

  3 cups brown sugar
  4 cups oats
  2 ½ tablespoons cinnamon
  1 teaspoon vanilla extract
  ½ tablespoon grated nutmeg
  ½ pound butter, softened
  4 - 5 pounds good cooking apples
  1 ½ quarts cold water
  juice of 1 lemon

Preheat oven to 350 degrees F.

Mix sugar, oats, cinnamon, vanilla extract, nutmeg and soft butter thoroughly. It should stick together without much pressure.

Peel and core apples and drop into lemon water until ready to use. Chop into bite-sized pieces and place them in a cobbler dish. Cover completely with prepared topping.

Bake for fifteen minutes, then turn pan ninety degrees. Check and turn every five minutes until top starts to brown. Remove to bakers rack and cool.

(8 servings)

Recipe courtesy of Mike Vitiello, Hurricane Kate's, Old Town Eureka

The pears in this recipe must be hot in order to flambé them, but they cannot be reheated without losing integrity. Therefore, they must be prepared just before serving. The ginger crème anglaise, however, may be made a day ahead and kept refrigerated.

Bourbon Flambéed Pears with Ginger Crème Anglaise
 2 cups heavy cream
 1/4 cup chopped fresh ginger
 1/3 cup, plus one cup, sugar
 6 egg yolks
 4 red d'anjou pears
 3 cups water
 3 - 4 anise stars
 1/4 cup brown sugar
 1 tablespoon butter
 4 ounces bourbon

   In a small stainless steel saucepan with a heavy bottom, combine heavy cream and chopped fresh ginger. Bring to a simmer over medium heat, then turn heat off and let it sit, covered, for ten to fifteen minutes.
   In a heat-proof mixing bowl, combine egg yolks and 1/3 cup sugar. Beat with a whisk until thoroughly blended.
   Pour the cream through a fine-mesh sieve to strain out bits of ginger. Add the strained cream to the yolks, a bit at a time, beating continuously with a whisk, until all the solids are dissolved.
   Transfer the mixture back into a clean saucepan, over medium-low heat, stirring constantly with a wooden spoon. Let simmer a few minutes until the sauce thickens and will coat a spoon.
   Remove from heat, transfer to a bowl, and refrigerate.
   Peel the pears. Cut them in half lengthwise, removing core and stems.
   In a large, shallow stainless steel bowl, combine the water, sugar and anise stars. Stir with a wooden spoon, making sure all the sugar is dissolved, then bring syrup to a boil. Carefully place the pears, one by one, in the hot liquid.

Simmer over medium-low heat until pears are tender, but not mushy. Turn off the heat, remove pears from the syrup and let stand at room temperature.

In a large non-stick pan, melt butter over medium heat.

Place the pears, flat side down, in the pan and let brown slightly, about two minutes.

Add the brown sugar and cook, turning pears as necessary to coat with the sugar. Remove the pan from the heat.

Have the bourbon in a glass. Pour from the glass into the pan. Return pan to heat and use a barbecue starter to ignite. When all the alcohol has burned off, serve pears with ginger crème anglaise.

(8 servings)

Recipe courtesy of Chef Alex Begovic, Personal Caterer, Eureka

Cow Butts, Humboldt County Fair   © *Matthew Filar*

CHAPTER FIVE

DAIRY PRODUCTS

The scenery southwest of Eureka soothes the soul. Between the bay and the highway, dairy farms, evergreen from a generous annual rainfall and frequent fog, hold gently to the road's edge. Cattle share the territory amicably with graceful egrets and indulge, at will, their cravings for grass and clover that form the basis for superior milk products.

It has been this way for well over a hundred years.

In the late nineteenth century, when economic and political hard times hit Scandinavia, waves of immigrants washed upon the shores of Humboldt Bay. While many of the new arrivals went to work in the timber industry, a number of them, notably the Danes, turned to dairy farming and found the area ideal for the pursuit.

Today, mailboxes along the Eel River still bear names like Christensen, Eriksen and Rasmussen. By the turn of the twentieth century, a number of families made their own cheese, and factories that produced cream cheese, cheddar and Swiss, sprang up as far north as Orick. One old-timer recounts that the Swiss cheese was of such excellent quality that, in 1920, a ready market was actually found for it in Switzerland.

Presently, Humboldt Creamery, on the banks of the Eel River, hums with activity, turning out two and a half million pounds of milk powder each month, along with butter, cottage cheese, a variety of milks, and two million pounds of ice cream annually made to the specifications of twenty-five different labels.

If you cross historic Fernbridge at the creamery, and drive through five more miles of dairy land, the road will bring you to "The Victorian Village of Ferndale," site of an annual mid-summer Scandinavian festival, Humboldt's County Fair, and the wild and whacky, world-famous Kinetic Sculpture Race. Discovered by Hollywood, Ferndale has served as the setting for films including *Salem's Lot*, *Outbreak*, and *The Majestic*. But the town's major claim to fame lies in the fact that the entire village has received Historical Landmark Status by the State of California.

Over the years, entrepreneurs have converted a number of the larger old homes, affectionately called "Butterfat Palaces" by residents of "The Cream City," into bed and breakfast accommodations. Johansens, international publisher of guides to travel lodgings, named one of these, The Gingerbread Mansion Inn, "the Most Excellent Inn in North America" for the year 2001.

A short walk from the picturesque center of town, the inn presides regally over a large corner at the intersection of Berding and Brown Streets. The tri-color Victorian presents an ornately carved display of spindles, gables and turrets to passersby. For those who venture inside, the charm continues. The front parlors and dining room bring the visitor into a quieter, more exquisitely detailed era of elaborate craftsmanship and comfortable grace. Beyond, eleven individually styled guest suites feature fine period furnishings enhanced by floral carpets, stained glass, authentic wallpaper, and Battenberg lace comforters. Little wonder the inn, built in 1899, has garnered such coveted recognition.

The inn's chef Larry Martin, a fifth-generation resident of the area and winner of many awards in his own right, has been featured on PBS cooking shows "Inn Country USA" and "Country Inn Cooking with Gail Greco." His interest in food dates back to childhood memories of his Danish great-grandmother's butter cookies. The silver-haired Martin, elegant in his black chef's tunic, fits well into his setting. His dark eyes twinkle as he recalls growing up in Ferndale. "A lot of my friends were little old ladies," he says with an easy smile. "I've always loved history, and many of these women were among the first generation to be born here. They had great stories to tell. And of course, they were marvelous cooks.

" The community had a lot of potlucks where everyone brought their best creations. We were always asking, 'Who made this?' and 'Can I get the recipe for that?'" His cookbook, *Cooking at the Inn with Chef Larry Martin* echoes those times with titles like "Erla's Prune Ladder," "Ida's Portuguese Sweet Rolls," and"Dora's Lemon Chiffon Pie."

While he claims no formal education in the culinary arts, the hours he spent in his grandparents' candy store, his part-time food service jobs growing up, and his innate love of cooking – especially baking – qualified him to take over the inn's generous kitchen when the opportunity arose. Former owner Ken Torbert wanted to move from a simple Continental breakfast to something more substantial, and Martin, who tended the inn's lush English gardens at the time, moved inside.

"We added quiches, soufflés and frittatas. In those days, I did the shopping, the cooking, the serving and the clean up. It was more than a full time job." Before long, Torbert suggested a fuller afternoon tea menu as well. "Now," Martin says, "we have an elaborate tea with a variety of sweet and savory dishes."

In 2002, Torbert sold the inn to Tom Amato and Maggie Dowd. Dowd, a chef trained at the Culinary Institute of America, works with Martin expanding the menus even further. He still reigns in the kitchen while she manages the beautifully appointed dining room.

Asked what makes the inn's food so special, he answers without hesitation. "We have so many wonderful fresh local ingredients. I use brown eggs that I get from a lady who raises chickens just two blocks from here. The Ferndale Meat Company around the corner makes over two dozen varieties of sausage, and we use many of them. We get cheese from the Loleta Cheese Factory and chevre from Cypress Grove – both national award winners many times over. And, of course, lots of fresh butter and cream from the Humboldt Creamery right down the road.

"The farmers markets have splendid produce. I shop there regularly. I even grow loganberries, boysenberries and rhubarb. The guests love it when I can tell them that I picked what they're eating from my own garden that very morning."

A block and a half away, in the Victorian Inn, Curley's Grill serves some of the best food around. Curley Tait grew up in a restaurant. At ten years old he was making salads with his friend Lorraine Blue in her father's Illinois restaurant. Later, Curley and Lorraine opened their own night club, Mother Blue's, in Chicago's Old Town. That career got side-tracked, however, when he left to manage the musical group, Spanky and Our Gang, a move that ultimately dropped him off in Los Angeles. The group dissolved, and Curley, burnt out from life in the fast lane, took his five-year-old son Adam, hit Highway 101, and headed north. They stopped when they got to Ferndale.

Curley went into and out of the restaurant business until 1995 when he opened Curley's Grill in a small Main Street storefront. The public response was huge. While Ferndale is definitely a tourist destination, it was not heavily weighted in restaurants. Since he opened, Curley has been enthusiastically covered in _Best Places in Northern California, Fodor's, Frommers,_ and periodicals from the _San Jose Mercury News_ to _Glamour Magazine._

In 2000, the Grill moved into the larger quarters where Curley currently holds court. Now, at seventy, he admits that pleasing people is still the impetus that drives him. He breeds, raises and trains Arabian horses, and he teaches Jazzercise in Arcata twice a week. He discusses both avocations with deep and abiding fervor. But it's the satisfaction of his customers at the Grill that dots the exclamation point of his life.

Susan Quinn, the restaurant's manager describes the Grill's success: "It's a coming together of Humboldt County and international cuisine. Everyone here has a passion for food and service. We have an open kitchen, so the cooks can watch the diners' expressions to make sure they're enjoying the experience."

Curley modestly attributes his success to his staff. He encourages chef Doug Hendricks and his cooks to invent specials. He and Hendricks developed the current menu together, and from January to June every year they feature a geographic area each month to add to the Thursday menus. Scandinavian, Caribbean, Thai, Spanish – the door is open to input from the youthful staff. It's not just the customers Curley wants to be happy. He designed the restaurant to provide a workplace where his employees can relish what they do, and he takes genuine joy in watching the young people he hires blossom.

How would he describe the Grill? He sees it as a blend of California cuisine and comfort food – and always, it's about making people happy. He makes sure that when families come in, the menu offers something for every age group. He provides options for vegetarians. And he offers a six-page catering menu that he customizes to guarantee customer satisfaction.

From the delectable menu options, to the curtained privacy booths he designed, to the open kitchen that allows instant customer feedback, Curley's Grill is all about feeling good.

In another arena, in 1978, a Eureka High School agriculture student asked his teacher Bob Laffranchi, "How do they make cheese?" Laffranchi sent the student to buy a book on the subject. The next day, another student brought in milk from his family's dairy. Thus armed, the entire class headed for the concession stand at the high school stadium where they used the range to make cheese – with abysmal results.

The following year, Laffranchi's next class repeated the experiment. Students wondered why the county, with so many dairies, had no cheese factory. Laffranchi and his wife Carol wondered the same thing. They began an investigation that, four years later, evolved into a wealth of information and an idea for a small, friendly cheese-making business much like the boutique wineries they had visited in Napa and Sonoma counties.

Loleta, a hamlet seven miles north of Ferndale and twelve miles south of Eureka, in the heart of the county's dairy country, turned out to be the ideal site. They purchased an historic, four-thousand square foot redwood shop in the center of town and began converting it to match their dream.

The family, including two elementary school-aged daughters, also took up residence in a seven-hundred-fifty square foot apartment above the shop. "We found ourselves," Carol says with a wry smile, "living like something lifted from the 1947 Claudette Colbert-Fred McMurray film, *The Egg and I,* right down to hatching chickens in our bedroom."

Looking around the light, spacious, convenience-filled kitchen she uses now, it's hard to imagine the primitive, pre-renovation quarters that once filled the same space. Downstairs, the shop reflects an equally amazing transformation.

The exterior still shows off its rustic redwood beginnings. Today, however, visitors pass through the front door into a tasting and sales room. Three large picture windows pull viewers into watching as great troughs of curds are changed by hand into award-winning cheese in a carefully controlled environment. A refrigerated case offers samples of selected varieties of their product: smoked salmon Monterey jack cheese, for example; jalapeno cheddar;

havarti; fontinas; a delicate, pure white, preservative-free queso fresco.

At the opposite end of the room a similar case carries choice cheeses of different types from other manufacturers. The knowledgeable and small-town friendly staff will answer questions, ring up sales, or just pass a pleasant time of day.

Beyond a gift shop with mustards, jams and sauces of every description, and a small but sophisticated selection of wines, lures food lovers. And for those who can't wait to get their purchases home, beautifully landscaped gardens provide a perfect place to picnic. Carol hopes, ultimately, to add a bistro and a space where other local food producers and chefs can demonstrate their techniques.

Meanwhile, it turns out, fortuitously, that Bob has a genuine talent for the complex process of cheese-making. When they began production in 1982, they hired two young women from Utah State University's dairy production program to advise and assist. Utah dairies are largely comprised of Holsteins whereas the milk Bob used came from Jerseys. The difference required adjustments in proportions, rennet, bacterial cultures and cooking times. But he worked on the recipes and by December of that year, The Loleta Cheese Factory opened its doors to the public, offering Creamy Monterey Jack and Mild Cheddar.

Today, the factory produces two and a half million pounds of cheese per year, in six varieties, for a total of thirty-one different flavors. Two hundred tons of this qualifies for organic certification. Laffranchi encourages staff members to come up with ideas for new flavors and to experiment. The rich, savory Roasted Garlic Monterey Jack, for example, sprang from staff inspiration. The finished product appears in the tasting room, and the Laffranchis get instant customer feedback on its marketability.

The system obviously succeeds. Since 1987, the Loleta Cheese Factory products have consistently taken some of the top honors in the American Cheese Society's annual competitions. Additionally, the fontina made at Loleta finds its way into Wolfgang Puck's frozen pizzas.

In 1998, the Laffranchis acquired their first dairy herd on a ranch in the nearby Ferndale Valley. The herd now numbers four-hundred-fifty milking cows – mostly Jerseys with some Holsteins – and it meets fifty per cent of their milk supply. In 2003, they added a Holstein dairy in Loleta, a few short blocks from the factory. Queso Fresco must be made from white milk like that the Holsteins produce. Jerseys don't fully metabolize the carotene in clover grass and so they give a milk that shows a creamier color. The amplified herd at the second dairy should supply enough milk to produce all six-hundred-thousand pounds of the Queso Fresco they sell annually.

Bob Laffranchi speaks of some day creating a demonstration dairy so that visitors can view the process from grazing through milking and cheese-making to the packaged finished product. Carol, whose passion lies in creating the site where it all happens, looks forward to the bistro project and still undreamed-of features which will maximize the experience for their guests. Meanwhile, Loleta Cheese Factory products reach an ever-expanding market.

On the southern edge of Eureka, at the top of Humboldt Hill, My Time Ranch is a goat farmstead with an ocean view. Owner Ginger Olsen breeds the goats, births the goats and raises the goats – ninety-two milking goats in all – to supply her customers with hand-made and hand-thrown cheese created in the early California style.

Ginger bought her first three goats twenty years ago because she was allergic to cow's milk. "But," she says, "the goats multiplied. When I got to six milkers, I bought a portable milking machine and started selling the surplus to Mary Keehn at Cyprus Grove."

In 1998, she and her partner at the time, Diana Livingston, made their first cheese and it was, Olsen declares emphatically, *a disaster!* But they kept at it, and in 2002, they decided to enter their Capricious Cheese in the American Cheese Society's annual competition. With four-hundred-sixty seven entries including goat, cow and sheep milk cheeses, the judges declared Capricious the Best Farmstead Cheese and the Best of Show.

Orders began pouring in and My Time Ranch stretched itself to keep pace. Output leapt from three hundred to twelve hundred pounds per week, and expects to soon double again. Although the partnership has since dissolved, the farmstead now employs a ranch manager and a cheese manager, and has added other cheeses including a feta to its line.

Olsen explains, "Feta was the first cheese, developed as a way of preserving milk. It's heavily salted and stored in brine, so it needs to be rinsed before serving. You rinse it, and then taste it. If its still too salty, you rinse it again. My personal preference is three rinses."

Presently, Olsen uses a one-hundred-gallon vat to pasteurize the milk, but with the surge in production, she's seeking to replace the vat with something five times that size. She pasteurizes at low temperature for a long time. The cheese is then drained, pressed between cypress boards and put to age in a "cave," a multi-chambered temperature-controlled structure where it is continually exposed to ocean breezes.

"The secret behind cheese is keeping the mold at an exact level which means continually scrubbing the cheese, the boards, the walls, everything. Karen, the cheese manager, is fantastic. She knows and loves each of the cheeses I age. And she expects her staff to work as hard as she does. That means ten per cent cheese-making and ninety per cent scrubbing. It's hard work, but it's absolutely essential for a quality finished product."

When a product stands on its own, you can enjoy it without a lot of frills. Ginger delights in cutting an ounce or two to have with a cup of tea or a glass of wine. And she religiously saves the trimmings and hardened bits that form around the edges. "You just toss them in casseroles, salads, pastas, anything. I haven't found anything they don't improve."

Continue north for about fifteen miles, and exit onto a narrow lane in rural McKinleyville. There, two unimposing and unmarked buildings house the space where Mary Keehn lives beyond her dreams. You might think something about her should shout success, but she seems as unassuming as the woman in front of you in line at the supermarket or the post office. Nothing suggests that she and her daughter, Malorie McCurdy, head up Cypress Grove Chevre, producing one of the best known, most sought after, and most highly honored goat cheeses in the world.

It's been a long, winding road. When Keehn finished her education in Santa Barbara, she longed for a place less densely populated, and moved north incrementally until, like others of her generation, she landed in Humboldt

County.

When Malorie was born in 1970, Keehn bought a goat to provide a source of safe, digestible milk. "Goats are easier than cows, " she says simply. "They take up less space, and they consume less food." As an outgrowth of her husbandry, she began making cheese.

Initially, only her family and select friends enjoyed the results. But as health-conscious consumers learned the benefits of goat cheese (typically it has half the fat found in cheese from cow's milk) the demand grew. In 1983, when her friend Dixie Gorrell decided to open the now upscale Larrupin Café, she proposed that Keehn provide goat cheese for the restaurant. The rest, as they say, is history.

Keehn's skill and ingenuity make for an ever-expanding line. At this writing, Cypress Grove sells a dozen different products with more in the works. Current offerings range from the fresh, light Fromage Blanc, winner of five gold medals in national competitions, to the sharp, smooth Goat Milk Cheddar, equally honored. The best known, Humboldt Fog, a light and creamy cheese with a center layer of vegetable ash, is as inviting to the eye as to the palate. Its sales average five hundred wheels a week. Newcomer, Midnight Moon, firm, buttery and full-flavored, is aged a year before it goes to market. A panel of one hundred judges at the 2002 International Fancy Food and Confection Show named it "Best New Product" in a competition open to twenty-three hundred exhibitors from fifty-one nations.

What makes Cypress Grove products so outstanding? Keehn names two reasons with certainty in her tone. "First, we all love what we do here. How many people can say that? And we put a high premium on quality ingredients. We lab test the milk weekly, and we pay a bonus to suppliers whose milk is exceptional in some way– a higher protein content, for example."

Keehn no longer raises goats herself. The cheese-making end of the business takes all of her time. But she praises her staff, which now numbers twenty-five, a giant step beyond her start as a young mother with a goat. And she praises the suppliers whose product quality she depends on as well.

Like Ginger Olsen, she proclaims the versatility of goat cheese. "My favorite way to eat it is plain, or spread on toast with a little marmalade. But it really goes with almost everything. Recently I was working up some recipes and I literally pulled everything in my kitchen out and tried it with the chevre. I couldn't believe how adaptable it is. It works with curries, with chutney, with almost anything."

NORTH COAST WAYS WITH DAIRY PRODUCTS

Chef Larry Martin generously shares some of his recipes, in the same spirit of neighborliness typical of his Ferndale upbringing. This recipe, put together the night before, is a great way to jump start busy mornings.

Savory Sausage Soufflé
cooking spray
3 slices white bread, cubed
3 slices whole wheat bread, cubed
1 pound sausage
1 teaspoon anise seed
1 ½ cups cheddar cheese, shredded
6 eggs
2 3/4 cups milk
1 teaspoon dry mustard
1/4 teaspoon oregano, crushed
1/4 teaspoon basil, crushed
1/4 teaspoon salt
1/8 teaspoon pepper

Grease six small ramekin dishes with cooking spray. Mix together white bread cubes with whole wheat bread cubes. Fill dishes half full with combined cubes.

Sauté the sausage with anise seed until brown. Drain well and divide between the ramekin dishes. Cover each dish with shredded cheddar and top with the remaining bread cubes.

Lightly beat eggs. Add milk and the remaining seasonings. Mix well and pour into the ramekin dishes, filling almost to the top. Cover and refrigerate overnight.

Preheat oven to 350 degrees. Uncover ramekin dishes and bake thirty minutes. (6 servings)

Recipe courtesy of Chef Larry Martin, Gingerbread Mansion Inn, Ferndale from Cooking at the Inn with Chef Larry Martin

Another of Chef Larry Martin's popular dishes that starts the night before, this simple polenta is flexible enough to serve at breakfast or dinner.

Baked Polenta

    1 clove garlic, minced
    4 cups chicken broth
    1 cup polenta
    4 tablespoons butter, plus 2 tablespoons for topping
    1/4 cup shredded cheddar cheese
    1/4 cup grated Parmesan cheese, plus 2 tablespoons for topping
    butter-flavored cooking spray

In a large pan over high heat, add garlic and broth. Bring to a boil. Stirring continuously, add polenta gradually. Reduce heat and boil gently, continuing to stir, until the mixture becomes thick and pulls away from the sides of the pan (about twenty to thirty minutes). Add butter and cheeses, stirring to combine thoroughly.

Spray a 5"x 9" loaf pan with cooking spray. Pour polenta mixture into pan. When cool, cover and refrigerate overnight.

Preheat oven to 350 degrees F.

Remove polenta from pan and cut into 3/4 inch thick slices. Spray a shallow casserole dish and place the slices in the dish, overlapping. Pour remaining melted butter over the top and sprinkle with Parmesan cheese. Bake, uncovered, thirty minutes. Serve hot.

(12 slices)

Recipe courtesy of Chef Larry Martin, Gingerbread Mansion Inn, Ferndale

Betty Burton, an excellent hostess who entertains frequently, says "I love using Loleta Cheeses for these spreads. The texture of their cheese is rich and creamy. It makes a wonderful appetizer or a great hostess gift. You can use regular cheddar or any combination of your favorite cheeses that go well with beer.

Crocked Beer Cheese

1 ½ teaspoons finely chopped garlic
1 teaspoon hot pepper sauce
1 tablespoon Worcestershire sauce
½ teaspoon dry mustard
½ teaspoon salt
3/4 cup (12 ounces)freshly grated smoked cheddar cheese
1/4 cup (4 ounces) freshly grated caraway seed jack cheese
1 cup Eel River Blonde Ale (If you aren't lucky enough to get
    Humboldt County Beer, go for your favorite.)
8 ounces cream cheese with chives

In the bowl of a food processor, whirl the garlic, hot pepper sauce, Worcestershire sauce, dry mustard and salt.

Add the cheese and slowly pour in the beer with the motor running.

Add the cream cheese and blend till smooth.

Pack in a mold or earthen crock. Cover and refrigerate at least twenty-four hours.

Serve with your favorite crackers, Belgian endive and vegetable sticks. For low carb diets, it's great with pork rinds.

Recipe courtesy of Betty Burton, Hostess, KINS Kitchen, and Perennial Oyster Festival Judge

This is another of Betty Burton's cheese spreads. She notes that it will last for two to three weeks in the refrigerator – if there's any left.

Mexican Crock Cheese
> 1/4 cup minced onion
> 1 clove garlic, minced
> 3 tablespoons butter
> 2 10-ounce cans diced tomatoes and green chilies
> 1/4 teaspoon black pepper
> 1/4 teaspoon salt
> 3 tablespoons diced green chilies
> 1 pound grated Monterey jack jalapeno cheese
> 1 pound grated jalapeno cheddar cheese
> 1 teaspoon Worcestershire sauce

Sauté the onions and garlic over medium heat until the onion is limp.

Add tomatoes, pepper and salt. Simmer over low heat 25 to 35 minutes. Remove from heat, add diced chilies and mix well.

Place cheeses in a mixing bowl and add the chile mixture and Worcestershire sauce. Blend thoroughly with a wooden spoon. Taste, and add salt if needed.

Pack into a 4 cup serving container or crock. Cover with plastic wrap, then add lid. Refrigerate twenty-four hours before serving.

Recipe courtesy of Betty Burton, Hostess, KINS Kitchen Perennial Judge, Oyster Festival

Mary Keehn's customers often send her recipes they've developed using Cypress Grove products and she generously passes them along. This is one such recipe. It is written as a main course, but could easily serve six or eight as a first course.

Portabella Dumplings with Goat Cheese Sauce

For the Dumplings
   3 tablespoons balsamic vinegar
   1/4 cup extra virgin olive oil
   1 tablespoon minced garlic
   salt and pepper to taste.
   1/4 teaspoon crushed red pepper flakes
   3 large portabella mushroom caps
   3 ounces chevre
   5 green onions, sliced thin
   24 wonton skins
   1 tablespoon butter

Mix together the vinegar, oil, salt, pepper and red pepper flakes.

Remove stems from mushrooms and marinate caps in oil mixture thirty minutes.

Remove caps from marinade and grill over coals or on a grill pan four minutes on each side. Dice the caps finely and mix well with chevre and onions.

Place a heaping tablespoon of this mixture in the center of a wonton skin. Moisten edges of the skin with water and fold into a triangle, pressing edges together to seal. Moisten tips of long ends and press together to form a dumpling.

Repeat this process until all the ingredients are formed into dumplings.

For the Sauce

  2 teaspoons butter
  1 shallot, finely chopped
  1 cup white wine
  1 cup heavy cream
  3 ounces chevre
  finely minced parsley for garnish
  finely chopped roasted red bell pepper for garnish

In a sauté pan over medium-low heat, melt the butter, add the shallot and sauté just until the shallot is limp.

Add the wine and reduce until thick and syrupy.

Add the cream and reduce until the sauce is two-thirds its original volume.

Add the cheese and stir until completely smooth.

Ladle a small amount of sauce onto each of four dinner plates. Arrange six dumplings on sauce, and decorate with remaining sauce. Garnish with finely minced fresh parsley and finely chopped roasted red bell pepper.

Serve immediately.

(4 main course portions)

Recipe courtesy of Mary Keehn, Proprietress, Cypress Grove Chevre, McKinleyville

Ed Chapman, Mary Keehn's stepfather, creates wonderful ways to use chevre. This invention is simple to prepare, and a joy both to see and to taste.

Ed Chapman's Pasta with Goat Cheese and Roasted Red Pepper Sauce
1 pound fettuccine (or pasta of your choice)
3 tablespoons salt
1 tablespoon olive oil
2 large red bell peppers, roasted, peeled and seeded
1 cup fresh parsley, no stems, tightly packed
10 ounces unflavored chevre
½ cup grated Parmesan cheese
3/4 cup toasted pine nuts

Cook the pasta in boiling water with salt and oil according to package directions.

Meanwhile, place parsley in a food processor and pulse eight to ten times. Add the roasted peppers and puree. Add cheeses and blend until smooth.

Drain the pasta and return it to the pot. Top with sauce, place over low heat and toss with pine nuts until well blended and heated through.

Serve immediately. Pass additional Parmesan cheese if desired. (4 servings)

Recipe by Ed Chapman, courtesy of Mary Keehn, Proprietress, Cypress Grove Chevre, McKinleyville

If you don't have a panini pan, you can use a grill pan for the bottom. Place your sandwich in the grill pan and top it with a heavy (cast iron, if you have it) skillet. Preheat the grill before you start cooking. Keep the heat just a little above medium. Cook the sandwich for nine minutes on the first side, flip and cook the second side until grilled to your taste. Bread will be crunchy, but the cheese will be melted and warm inside.

Grilled Vegetable Panini

    4 cibatta rolls, split in half lengthwise
    4 ounces of Purple Haze Chevre at room temperature
    1 eggplant, sliced thin and grilled
    2 red bell peppers, roasted, peeled, seeded, and cut into large chunks
    1 8-ounce jar marinated artichoke hearts, drained, reserving liquid
    1 large fresh tomato, thinly sliced
    1 cup fresh spinach leaves, chiffonade
    salt, pepper, and crushed red pepper to taste

Spread ½ ounce cheese on cut edges of each roll. Cover the bottom layer with eggplant slices. Cover the eggplant with a layer of red bell peppers.

Cut each artichoke heart into eighths and spread over the peppers. Cover the artichoke hearts with tomato slices.

In a mixing bowl, toss spinach in several teaspoons of the reserved artichoke marinade and the seasonings. Put 1/4 of the spinach mixture on each sandwich.

Place top layers of rolls on each sandwich, cheese-side down. Brush outsides, lightly, top and bottom, with extra virgin olive oil and grill in a panini pan until cooked through.

(4 panini)

Recipe courtesy of Mary Keehn, Proprietress, Cypress Grove Chevre, McKinleyville

Many of our local chefs have outdone themselves in working with local dairy products. Alex Begovic came up with this out-of-this-world treatment. He says that the trick to successful crepes is to use a high quality non-stick pan or, even better, a cast iron pan with a thoroughly seasoned patina.

Cypress Grove Goat Cheese Blintzes with Radicchio Salad and Lemon Vinaigrette

For the Crepes:
   3 eggs at room temperature
   1 ½ cups milk at room temperature
   1 cup all-purpose flour
   ½ teaspoon salt
   2 tablespoons melted butter

In a medium mixing bowl, beat eggs until smooth.

Add milk and stir until well-blended.

Whisk in flour and salt, mixing thoroughly. Strain the batter through a fine-mesh sieve, and whisk in the melted butter. Let the batter rest at room temperature for one hour.

When you are ready to make the crepes, mix the batter well. Using a small ladle, pour about ½ ounce (a bit more than one tablespoonful) into a lightly buttered, small non-stick pan over medium heat. Swirling the pan to coat with the batter, cook until the crepe is slightly golden brown on both sides.

Repeat until all batter is used. You should have about twenty crepes. Cool them at room temperature, then proceed with the filling.

For Goat Cheese Filling:
   1 ½ cups Cypress Grove Chevre (or high quality substitute)
   ½ cup ricotta cheese
   3 tablespoons fresh chopped chives
   1 tablespoon finely grated orange zest (or lemon zest)
   1 teaspoon sugar
   2 teaspoons salt

   Preheat the oven to 400 degrees F.
   In a large bowl, mix all ingredients thoroughly. Do not use a food processor for this step. It breaks down the goat cheese.
   Spoon out about two tablespoons of the filling and place it in the center of a crepe. Fold the crepe, enclosing the filling completely, and place on low-rim or rimless baking sheet. Bake in preheated oven ten to fifteen minutes, to warm –not heat – the filling.
   While the crepes bake, make the

Lemon Vinaigrette:
   1/4 cup freshly squeezed lemon juice
   ½ cup olive oil
   2 tablespoons sugar
   1/4 tablespoon salt

   Place all ingredients in a blender and process until emulsified.

For Presentation:

    radicchio and Belgian endive

    additional finely minced orange zest and chopped fresh chives for garnish

- OR -

    freshly cracked black pepper and fresh parsley, finely chopped for garnish

    Using eight salad plates, make cups of radicchio and/or endive. Place two warm blintzes on each plate. Drizzle with vinaigrette, garnish and serve immediately.

    (8 first course servings)

Recipe courtesy of Chef Alex Begovic, Personal Caterer, Eureka

Chef Paul Clarke uses fresh farmers market produce and Humboldt Fog Chevre to make this spectacular salad. If you have trouble finding some of the beet varieties, use whatever is fresh in your area. Roasting gives the beets a better texture and brings out the natural sweetness in them. Use a disposable towel to rub them; they will stain. And dress them while they are still warm. They will absorb more of the flavor.

Roasted Three Beet Salad with Humboldt Fog Chevre and Arugula

    4 red beets, washed
    4 golden beets, washed
    4 Chiogga beets, washed
    1 cup olive oil
    1/3 cup red wine vinegar
    1/4 cup Dijon mustard
    2 tablespoons sugar
    salt and pepper to taste
    4 tablespoons finely chopped parsley
    2 bunches arugula
    1 pound Humboldt Fog Chevre

Preheat the oven to 400 degrees F.

Rub the beets with a little of the oil and season with salt and pepper. Roast for forty to forty-five minutes. While they are still warm, use a disposable towel to rub off the skins.

Mix remaining oil, vinegar, mustard, sugar and 2 tablespoons of the parsley.

Using separate bowls for each color beet, slice the beets and toss them with the dressing. Allow to chill for one hour.

Arrange the cheese, arugula and beets on chilled salad plates. Drizzle with dressing.

(4 salad servings)

Recipe courtesy of Chef Paul Clarke, The Groves at Riverbend, Myers Flat

This is a simple, yet elegant salad, from Chef Jeff Sesar. He makes a roasted garlic oil for the crostini by roasting six cloves of garlic in olive oil over medium heat until the garlic is a rich golden brown.

Mixed Baby Greens with Citrus Vinaigrette and Cypress Grove Chevre Crostini

For the Crostini:
    1 seeded baguette, sliced through on the bias
    roasted garlic oil (see note above)
    8 ounces Cypress Grove Chevre

    Preheat broiler.
    Brush the baguette slices on both sides with roasted garlic oil. Spread in a single layer on a baking sheet and toast lightly on both sides under the broiler about two minutes. Remove from broiler and spread with the chevre. Set aside.

For the Salad:
    3 navel oranges
    1 grapefruit
    2 lemons
    2 limes
    1/4 cup honey
    1 heaping tablespoon (2 ounces) shallots, minced
    1 tablespoon (1 ounce) garlic, minced
    2 ½ tablespoons (½ bunch) fresh basil
    3 ounces red wine vinegar
    1 tablespoon Dijon mustard
    salt and pepper to taste
    1 ounce sesame oil
    6 ounces extra virgin olive oil
    4 cups your choice of mixed baby greens

Whisk all ingredients except greens together, whisking after each addition. Whisk oils in last.

Arrange greens, drizzle with dressing and garnish with crostini.

Pass additional dressing at table. Leftover dressing will keep in the refrigerator for up to five days. (4 salads)

Recipe courtesy of Chef Jeff Sesar, Moonstone Grill, Trinidad

And, now, for dessert: Chef Larry Martin's recipe for Butter Bars, a sweet treat any time of the day. They really do melt in your mouth.

Melt In Your Mouth Butter Bars

For Butter Cake Layer:
1 ½ cups flour
1 ½ teaspoons baking powder
½ teaspoon salt
12 ounces unsalted butter, softened
3/4 cup sugar
2 large eggs at room temperature
1 1/4 teaspoons vanilla
½ cup whole milk

Generously butter a 12"x16" jelly roll pan and set aside.
Sift flour, baking powder and salt together.
In the large bowl of an electric mixer, using a whisk attachment, cream the butter and sugar together until light and fluffy, about three minutes.
Add eggs, one at a time, beating thoroughly after each addition.
Add the vanilla.
Spoon in the flour mixture alternately with the milk. Blend until the batter is smooth, being careful not to over mix. Pour the batter into the prepared pan.

For the Topping:
8 ounces cream cheese
2 large eggs
4 cups confectioner's sugar, sifted and divided
1/4 teaspoon almond extract
2 teaspoons vanilla extract
½ cup pecans, lightly toasted then finely chopped
2 ounces white chocolate, melted

Preheat the oven to 325 degrees F.

In the large bowl of an electric mixer, fitted with a paddle attachment, beat the cream cheese, eggs, 3 cups of the confectioner's sugar and the almond and vanilla extracts at low speed until smooth. Increase the speed to high and beat for five minutes. Reduce speed to low and add the remaining cup of sugar. Raise speed to high again and beat for five more minutes.

Pour the mixture over the butter cake layer and bake thirty-five to forty minutes until top is lightly browned. Remove pan from oven and place on a rack to cool for thirty minutes.

Drizzle melted chocolate decoratively over the top and sprinkle with nuts.

Chill in the refrigerator until the chocolate is completely set. Slice into bars with a knife, periodically running the knife under hot water.

Store in an airtight container.

(from 64 1"x3" bars to many more if cut smaller)

Recipe courtesy of Chef Larry Martin, Gingerbread Mansion Inn, Ferndale

Lost Coast Brewery © *Matthew Filar*

CHAPTER SIX

LIBATIONS

Beverages become increasingly important in dining. Food publications feature pairing articles, wine reviews and winery coverage. Culinary schools offer classes in the same subjects. While connoisseurs have long valued fine wine, and dedicated themselves to its pursuit, wine has become a recognized art form among growing numbers of the general public.

Additionally, the expanding numbers of micro-breweries around the nation cater to people who put ever greater importance on the quality of the beer they drink. Gone are the days when supermarket refrigerators stocked five or six brands with almost indistinguishable differences between them. Today dozens of labels with names ranging from funky to exotic entice aficionados some of whom are as passionate and as knowledgeable as their wine-fancying counterparts.

Humboldt County has jumped on the beverage bandwagon with both feet. Award wining wineries and micro-breweries spring up with exciting frequency, and locally bottled beverages can be found far from the county's confines. The people at the helm creating these local libations have paid their dues. They have mastered their subject and express commitment to turning out quality products. Judges at the competitions they have entered agree.

Briceland boomed in the early part of the twentieth century. Although the town had been laid out by John Briceland who settled there in 1889, it was Charles Wagner, a tanner by trade, who gets credit for expansion. Wagner founded The Wagner Leather Company in Stockton, California, and early in the twentieth century he purchased property in southern Humboldt County in order to utilize the great number of oak trees growing there. He built the Pacific Oak Extract Works which cut the trees, stripped the bark, extracted the tannin, boiled it down to a molasses-like consistency, and shipped it from Shelter Cove's wharf to San Francisco.

In its heyday the town boasted a population of some three hundred people, three hotels, two general stores, two saloons, a town hall, a school and a post office. What it did not have was a fire department, and in 1914, a fire swept through destroying everything on the north side of town. When the tanbark supply ran out in 1922, the Wagners shut down their business there, and the boomtown went bust.

While it never fully recovered, from 1968 to 1977, an influx of several hundred people found their way to the area. Variously called hippies, long hairs, and some terms not fit to print, the newcomers were disenchanted with the turn taken by the Great American Dream. They sought to re-invent that dream in this remote rural setting where they could buy land for very little money and live in a way they believed fit their system of values.

Maggie Carey and her husband Joe Collins were among the first to arrive. "We were hippie back-to-the-landers in those days," she says with a smile. "One of the first things we did here was put in a vegetable garden. We made our own beer, too. So when we had an opportunity to get grapes from a friend who was growing them in Mendocino, making wine seemed the next logical step.

"In 1976, we planted a few vines of our own just to see how they'd do. They thrived quite happily here. Friends liked the wine we made so much that they tried to get us to sell it to them. Of course, that would have been illegal, so in 1985, we got certified and became a business.

"We've got a great microclimate here. You can see how well the vineyards do up on the hills. By the river there's a frost problem, and the dampness tends to promote mold, but higher up the grapes grow beautifully.

"We grow some of the grapes we use, and we get a lot from friends with vineyards. All of the wines we make come from small family vineyards nearby except for the Sauvignon Blancs which come from Lakeport. We produce about two thousand cases a year, most of which goes to restaurants from Larrupin Café in Trinidad to the Benbow Inn, and to small, independent markets throughout the same area. Some of it leaves the county, though. We fill mail orders, and our Humboldt Brut is actually pretty popular in Napa."

Like all their wines, the champagne is made on the premises. "We started growing Pinot Noirs in anticipation of using the under- ripe grapes we were sure to have at times," Carey explains. "Our press is specifically designed for making champagne. Once pressed, the wine is stored in barrels for at least three years. Then we bottle it, add the yeast, and cap the bottles.

"The riddling, a process by which each bottle is stored horizontally and given a quarter of a turn at regular intervals, used to be done entirely by hand. Today, we can pack five hundred bottles into a large, wooden box, and load two boxes onto a machine that does the turning. When we calculated the man-hours we saved, we realized it was really cost-effective."

The winery's back wall, thickly hung with award ribbons, testifies to the quality of Briceland Vineyard Winery's output, which Carey would like to be able to label organic. "But in order to do that," she says with a trace of irritation, "I would have to pay to have the winery certified, and each grower that we use would have to pay to have his vineyard certified. There are new vineyards starting up all the time. My husband helps them set up, and does a lot of advising. We want to support them if they're good, but the fees are simply out of reach sometimes. We sidestep the issue by putting a disclaimer on the label that says, 'No synthetically compounded fertilizers, pesticides or herbicides have been used in the cultivation of these grapes.'

"That's important to me. Grapes don't hurt the land at all, and that's important to me as well. This business has been good to us. We've met a lot of wonderful people, and we've enjoyed tremendous community support.

"Increasing production would be tough. We're too close to the Napa Valley, and they're very well established down there. But Joe is an architect, so we're not under any pressure to get bigger."

Briceland Vineyard Winery hosts formal tastings twice each year. In 2003, they used one such event to introduce a new still wine, a 2001 Lost Coast Chardonnay, and a sparkling wine, a 1997 Reserve Rose Brut, in addition to pouring an assortment of their other varieties.

Putting Briceland Vineyards on your stock winery tour would lend a whole new meaning to the phrase "out of the way," but the wines are unquestionably worth it, and the denizens prove that, certainly for some, the pursuit of the re-configured American Dream has absolutely paid off.

Up the road a piece (in Humboldt County "the road" almost always refers to US 101) the Meagher brothers, Thomas and Michael, in a leap of faith, are expanding their investment in the area's potential. Using grapes developed at the University of California in Davis, they've planted thirty experimental acres, chosen the most successful varieties, and begun bottling and selling the results at their brand new Riverbend Winery in Myers Flat.

The Meaghers are not new to the wine-making venture. Tom has been a partner in Mendocino County's Pacific Star Winery for years. But this project is bigger and more comprehensive. It represents a commitment to bring back an earlier time in Southern Humboldt.

"Our father," Tom says, "retired from a career as a merchant seaman. He bought several night spots locally, ending up with the Myers Flat Saloon. In those days, this whole area was filled with campgrounds, motor courts and summer homes. That was prior to the popularity of air travel. The road ran through here, the river ran through here, and America traveled by car. People in Eureka and Arcata came here to escape the fog and cooler summer temperatures. It was easy to reach by car, the sun shone brightly, and you could always jump in the river to cool off.

"Today America is returning to the road. Airport security is a hassle, and people are nervous about the risks. Certainly most business trips and emergency travel will continue to be done by air, but car travel is experiencing a renaissance, and this is an ideal area for that to happen."

To that end, the Meaghers, Tom, Mike and Mike's wife Suzie, have opened A Taste of Humboldt, a commodious tasting room where visitors can sample Riverbend's products. This would be ambitious in itself, but their vision is huge. They have purchased and re-opened Knight's Restaurant as a site for breakfast and lunch and a brand new dinner house, The Groves at Riverbend.

To oversee the kitchens, they've hired Paul Clarke, a European-trained chef with impressive credentials. The son of a Dublin restaurateur, Clarke worked in London, Paris and Germany before coming to America in 1990. He started out in Minneapolis where he opened the first Le Cordon Bleu School of Cooking. But the Minneapolis environment didn't offer some of the things he felt were important.

"Admittedly, the criteria were high," Clarke explains. "I wanted to be near the ocean. I wanted to be near the forests. I wanted an even climate. And frankly, there aren't too many places that meet all those criteria." Humboldt County did.

Both Clarke and the Meaghers seem pleased to have come together in this venture. "I had a stack of resumes this high," Tom Meagher says, indicating a generous difference between thumb and forefinger. "But I knew right away that Paul was the person I wanted. We see food the same way. We think the same things are important."

For Clarke, who describes himself as "ingredient-driven," the venues provide an opportunity to express himself creatively in wonderful ways. One of the biggest adjustments he's had to make since coming to the United States involves working with American foodstuffs. "I discovered that many of the classic French recipes I'd been cooking for years just didn't work any more. The difference was in ingredients. Milk, for instance, has a much higher butterfat content in Europe than it does here. In Europe you can skim off the cream that rises to the top of a bottle of a bottle of milk. Here it's been pasteurized and homogenized. You can't even buy raw milk here. It's against the law.

"The staples here all reach the customer after they've been heat treated or enriched. That happens as a reaction to something. Children come down with an illness that indicates a vitamin D deficiency, and the manufacturers decide that they can sell more of their product by fortifying it with vitamin D.

"But all the processing really affects the way that ingredients react in recipes. It really impacts the taste." He's spent years working with his recipes. Using the techniques he mastered abroad and the ingredients now available to him, Clarke recreates the delectable flavors he seeks. Diners who stop at Myers Flat today expecting to find standard American road food come away from the table surprised and delighted by their experience.

In a quiet residential neighborhood on the outskirts of McKinleyville, vintners Michele (Mickey) Elaine and Dylan Gray work with a rare passion to produce fine red wines under their Lluvia label. "We got into this," Elaine asserts, "because we really love wine. We do everything by hand, sorting each bunch of grapes we use. Right now, we bring all of our grapes in from Napa, Sonoma and Amador Counties, but that may change in the future.

"No matter where the grapes are grown, we follow them throughout the growing season. *That* won't change. We want to know the history of what we use."

Elaine speaks softly, but with evident fervor. "When we find a wine we fall in love with," she says, "we contact the vintner. We arrange to visit the winery and do barrel tastings."

Gray adds, "We've had excellent relationships with other vintners. It's a tight-knit community, and very supportive. We've learned a lot from working with them."

"We read a lot of books," Elaine continues. "We've done a lot of research, and a lot of experimenting. One of best things in what we do is the opportunity to always keep learning and growing."

Even though they're relative newcomers to the field, they've already determined that their growth will be in the area of quality, not quantity. "Right now we produce four hundred to five hundred cases a year," Gray points out. "We don't want to go over one thousand."

Currently, they offer a Syrah, a Petit Syrah, a Merlot, a Cabernet Sauvignon, a Cabernet Blanc, a Sangiovese, and a late harvest Zinfandel Port. Some of the area's most prestigious restaurants have added Lluvia to their wine lists, and select local outlets now stock it on their shelves.

Inside the winery, deep purple fruit ferments in stainless steel vats. Every item from the sparkling glass bottles to the gleaming wood of the wine press reflects the careful attention to detail the young couple demands from themselves. "We pour our heart and soul into every bottle," Elaine says. It shows in the color, the aroma, and the flavor of their finished products.

The Cabernet Sauvignon, for example, carries the aromas and flavors of blackberries, raspberries and chocolate, with a suggestion of vanilla and minerals. Aging nearly two years in French and Hungarian oak creates a silky finish. The overall effect conveys a sense of subtle elegance.

The Merlot, similarly aged, presents the palate with a pleasant fruitiness:

black currant, blackberry and raspberry, with touches of blueberry and eucalyptus in the mix. It exudes the refinement of a quality wine.

The late harvest Zinfandel Port is one that any host would serve with pride. Its rich sweetness lets it stand alone as a dessert, or it could pair beautifully with fruit and cheese.

Finding a small label like Lluvia might take a bit of doing, but the effort will be richly rewarded. The care, the attention to detail, and the passion that these vintners lavish on their wines result in a product sure to receive high praise in the years ahead.

Several miles east, in the picturesque rural community of Fieldbrook, Bob and Judy Hodgson count themselves among the people who contributed to Lluvia's foundation. The Hodgsons came to Humboldt County when Bob accepted a teaching position in Humboldt State University's Oceanography Department. In the fall of 1976, they purchased a home in tiny Fieldbrook. The site they chose included generous grounds and a small lake.

Their family physician had taken up wine making as a hobby, and Bob Hodgson, a longtime lover of good wine, learned the vintner's craft from his doctor.

In 1978, the Hodgsons got certified, set up a winery in their garage and began making their own wines. When they decided to turn their hobby into a business, they purchased their grapes from outside the area. Then, in 1982, they connected with a grape grower in nearby Trinity County whose vineyards had already produced award winning wines. Two years later, the Merlot they produced from those grapes was named the best Merlot at the California State Fair. Today, except for a few Italian varietals, Hodgson uses grapes from Trinity, Mendocino and Humboldt counties in all his wines.

Making wine from Humboldt County grapes is a relatively new venture, but one that Fieldbrook Valley Winery has already proved can succeed. The 2000 Pinot Noir, from grapes grown at Phelps Vineyard in southern Humboldt, took a bronze medal at the 2003 Los Angeles County Fair. Hodgson relates that one expert at the event commented that it wasn't surprising the wine won an award. The surprise was that the grapes came from Humboldt County.

Over the years, the winery's physical setting began to develop. First, the Hodgsons realized the need for a forklift, so they built a full-fledged production facility with fourteen foot high ceilings to accommodate that. Their production grew from five hundred to two thousand gallons as a result. Currently their output runs at one thousand gallons, which is about as big as they choose to be. "We're smaller than small," Bob Hodgson says, "But this way we can stay on top of every barrel."

"It's easy to make wine. It's harder to sell wine," he continues. "We've seen good sales in cities around the nation. We've even sold our wine as far away as Tokyo. But since the World Trade Towers went down, a lot has changed, and our marketing has changed with it. Now the bulk of our sales is local."

He has recently formed a wine club which sends quarterly shipments of two to four bottles at a time according to member specifications. A newsletter apprises members of new releases and upcoming winery events, includes tasting notes and profiles of individuals who contribute to Fieldbrook Valley wines. Judy Hodgson also publishes *The North Coast Journal* , a widely respected local news magazine, and the newsletter, while small, is stamped by a professional quality in the Hodgson tradition.

The winery has also added its first full-time employee. Up until 2003, the Hodgsons, assisted by their two sons, did it all. Now with Fieldbrook Valley's reputation firmly established, Bob Hodgson says, "I want to have some fun. Wine making *is* fun, but now I have the freedom to travel as well."

Randy Ward, their new assistant wine maker, worked as a "cellar rat" at Fieldbrook Valley while he attended Humboldt State. After graduating, he became assistant wine maker at a Santa Cruz, California, operation. His recent return to Fieldbrook Valley made it possible for the Hodgsons to spend some time in Italy, learning about grape growing and wine making there.

Enhancing the winery aspect of their site, the Hodgsons built a stylish tasting room comfortable enough to live in while their home was being remodeled. They expanded the residence, adding a second floor and redesigning the exterior to resemble a French chateau. This, coupled with the serene setting, the beautifully landscaped grounds, and the lake, have made the Fieldbrook Valley site a popular spot for weddings.

"We only do about five weddings a year now," Hodgson says. "With everything else, it's just too much." The "everything else" refers to providing a venue for benefits for community organizations like the Humboldt Area Foundation and the Fieldbrook Foundation.

Hodgson points out that there are now some twenty-five vineyards in the county, and twenty small wineries, many of which are producing excellent wines. He's enthusiastic about the future of the business here, and confident about Fieldbrook Valley's place as a leader in the local industry.

It's hard to think of wine in Humboldt County without thinking of the nationally acclaimed 301 Restaurant. Visitors who have read glowing reviews of the spot may well be surprised when they first arrive. It's a small, intimate space, seating about thirty diners in all, but it boasts multi-course menus that change frequently to take advantage of seasonal bounty, a highly awarded wine cellar of thousands of bottles, and a reputation that draws guests from far and wide.

Mark and Christi Carter didn't exactly plan it that way. Mark insists that it all started with "the house," a three-story Victorian he built from plans drawn by top nineteenth century architects Joseph and Samuel Newsome.

"I thought I was getting out of construction," he muses. "We decided we'd build the house, move in, and raise lots of kids. It took three times as long as we figured, and ended up costing three times as much as we expected. By the time we were done, we had a couple of children and realized that was plenty. Then we had to come up with a way to make the house pay for itself."

At first they used it to showcase art and antiques they sold. A friend suggested that the house would lend itself well to a bed-and-breakfast, so they began renting out rooms on the top floor to paying guests. Christi, already an excellent cook, realized that many of those guests would be business people whose schedules might not allow for lunch, so the four-course Carter House Breakfast was born. Before long, _California Magazine_ labeled it "The best breakfast in the state."

Since they opened in 1982, Mark has bought and restored two residences next to the house and built a small hotel diagonally across the street. The staff has grown to forty people, some of whom have been with the family since they first began.

"We just hired a dining room manager," Carter says, seemingly surprised by the fact. "We never had a dining room manager before. But we've already seen our level of service upgraded."

They also have a full-time gardener on the staff. As with many of the county's dining spots, the emphasis at 301 hinges on "fresh," and much of the produce, herbs and edible flowers served in the restaurant grows right on the grounds in the large gardens or in the greenhouse.

Dinners initially were a fixed-price entree with accouterments, a system the well-traveled Carters knew and felt they could manage. Like the rest of their undertakings, however, this one has grown. In addition an *a la carte* menu, patrons can now select from a five-course Discovery Menu or an eight-course *Grand Chef Degustation* with a suggested wine flight paired to each course.

The wine is a story in its own right, one that Mark Carter warms up to with even more than his usual enthusiasm. "My grandfather," he says, "came from Italy, and wine was always a part of his meals. When we ate with him, we were served wine, too, so I developed an appreciation for it early in life.

"Over the years, I began buying it – at first for us to enjoy, and then, to be able to share with our guests. I like to serve wine. No one complains about it, because most people don't really know much about it. Everyone has always eaten, so everyone has an opinion about food. They'll order something off the menu, and then complain that it doesn't taste like it did when their grandmother used to make it.

"People don't do that with wine. Once in a rare while, someone will send a bottle of wine back because of cork problems. That happens, and you can see the problem at a glance. But it doesn't happen often."

Their cellars expanded to phenomenal proportions. Word got out, and *Wine Spectator* magazine showed up to verify the buzz. In recent years, the prestigious publication has consistently conferred their Grand Award "for being one of the finest wine lists in the world" on the inn.

To spread their joy, Mark Carter put together the 301 Wine Club. Each month he elects wines from the best new releases and from "rare library vintages" to send to members. As with the inn and the restaurant, his intention is to share his personal pleasures and add to the pleasures in others' lives. He structured the club so that memberships can be custom-tailored to individual preferences. Four tiers provide a broad price range, and deliveries include tasting notes, food pairing suggestions and recipes.

The only thing left seemed to be for Mark to become a vintner himself, and in 1998, Carter Cellars put up its first vintage. In partnership with the highly acclaimed winemaker Nils Venge, Carter is using grapes from select Napa Valley vineyards to produce prized Cabernet Sauvignon and Merlot. "Our focus is on quality, not quantity. We'll produce less than three hundred and fifty cases a year. That's not a lot, but it will be great."

With all this, what could the Carters possibly want for the future? "Just to maintain our standard, to be the very best. What we do here is just to share our lives with people, to help them enjoy a memorable experience."

It's working. Their AAA Four Diamond Awards each read, "to Carter House Inns, for providing exceptional guest accommodations, excellent service, and an elegant atmosphere," which just about says it all.

While the Carters have understandably sewn up the national press on coverage of their extensive wine offerings, other county restaurants with smaller cellars provide diners with admirable options. One such place is Folie Douce in Arcata's Northtown.

Wendy Day went to work waiting tables at Folie Douce, in 1992. The restaurant, an intimate spot, had only been open a year at the time. Day, who had waitressed at other venues in town, was drawn to the ambiance and the menu. When, in 1998, the original owners left to make wine in the Napa Valley, she bought them out to ensure that the place she'd come to love wouldn't change.

"I see it as a special little spot in the community," she says, "a mini-vacation for the people who come here." To that end, she's kept the essence of the restaurant intact. Customers enter the front door and are met by the open kitchen where chef Mike Stengl and his staff put together the imaginative food that highlights the frequently changing menu. Stengl started at Folie Douce in

1983. His food style has been an important part of what Day hoped to preserve.

"Our menu is, first of all, eclectic. I think of it as food you'd cook for yourself at home, but with a twist. For example, we do a filet mignon. You might do a filet mignon at home, but you might not think to try it with wasabi.

"The season determines much about what we serve. This area has a lot of good food year round. I hear people complain that California doesn't have seasons. But in this business I've realized that we *do* have seasons.

"Right now, it's early Spring. The rains have backed off, the temperature is warming up, and the mushrooms are wonderful. We've wrapped up the Dungeness crab season, and we're not quite ready for Farmers Market. Before long we'll start getting berries.   Soon after that, we'll have so much produce we won't have enough places to put it.

"After that, we get what used to be the hardest season of all for me: Autumn. But now I'm finding that's when all the great peppers are out there, and the winter squash starts coming in. It's wonderful! And, of course, the greens are good all year round. You just have to harvest different greens in different seasons. And all of it gives us here a chance to get creative.

"We do a lot of pizzas here in the wood-fired oven. We've found that anything you put on a sandwich will go on a pizza. You might not come up with salami and Brie with mozzarella and apricot jam, but if you try it on one of our pizzas, you might like it."

From first courses, which might include an artichoke heart cheesecake or a spinach salad with roasted duck leg confit, to main courses as unique as maple and mustard grilled pork tenderloin with wild mushrooms or the wasabi steak grilled with scallions and sesame seeds, the flavor combinations are lively and intriguing.

The setting reflects the same approach with sedate white table linens, bright, eclectic art on textured gold walls, and exposed beams wreathed in garlands of dried seed pods wrapped in strings of tiny white lights. In unexpected spots, whimsical touches engage the diners' attention: a silver metal flower bucket filled with fresh dill fronds; a black cache-pot holding foot-long ginger roots; a wrought iron basket showing off layered fresh lemons and limes. The impact is one of fine dining touched with a sense of humor.

"The staff spends long hours here," Day says, "and they work hard in tight quarters. It's important that things are not too serious."

What are her dreams? "At some point, I'd really like to go to sommelier school. I like educating the public, suggesting things for them to try and enjoying the satisfaction I feel when they like what I've suggested. I get to do that with food now, but it would be nice to feel confident doing it with wine as well."

The restaurant already boasts an award-winning wine list. It's hard to imagine improvement, but if anyone could that, it would probably be Wendy Day.

Meanwhile, in Eureka, micro-brewery fans have found a home at Lost Coast Brewery with Barbara Groom as their hostess/house-mother/server and/friend. Groom grew up on a farm outside Stockton, California. When time came to go to college, she paid her way through a pharmacy degree at Washington State University by raising pigs. "I was a junior capitalist from the get-go," she says with an easy laugh.

She did her internship in San Francisco. "I thought I wanted to be in the city because I'd been in the country so long. But in the early seventies, during the gas crisis, cars were lined up for blocks. Then both major supermarkets in the area got hit by strikes and we couldn't get anything to eat, and a lot of the glamour of city living flew out the window.

"So in 1977, I moved to Humboldt County, bought a house in Loleta, and went to work for an independently owned pharmacy. Then I realized that counting pills all day every day wasn't what I wanted to do either.

"In 1984, laws about micro-breweries finally changed. I was driving through Hopland, on the way to San Francisco, and I noticed that one of the buildings had a big sign on it that said 'Mendocino Brewing Company - Grand Opening.' I said to myself as I whizzed by, 'Hah! They can't do that!' But on the way back here I decided to check it out. I went into the brewery, and saw the big stainless steel vats, and smelled the brews fermenting, and instantly fell in love.

"I already liked beer. But what I found out was that I loved the whole fermentation thing. It's like magic. It turns grapes into wine, flour into bread, and barley and hops into beer. It's really great stuff."

She and partner Wendy Pound traveled extensively, visiting breweries and micro-breweries, learning all they could. Then, in 1990, they opened the Lost Coast Brewery in Eureka. "The first two years were really tough," Groom admits. "But I kept my nose to the grindstone and stuck it out. Not everyone can do that. My partner couldn't. I bought her out. I worked hard, tracked down financing, and by the end of the second year, the business was showing a profit."

Today she sits at her desk on the second floor of The Lost Coast Brewery Café, still looking like a fresh-faced farm girl, but wrapped in the self-assurance of a successful entrepreneur. In an era when micro-breweries are coming into their own, Lost Coast has grown to become the ninth largest in the nation.

The brewery, in its own warehouse several blocks away, pumps out five different beers bottled in six-pack format and two other varieties in twenty-two ounce bottles. Their awards pile up steadily. *All About Beer* magazine commissioned a panel of thirty beer experts to name their "must taste" beers of the world, and Lost Coast's Indica India Pale Ale made the list. The Raspberry Brown took the Best of California Award in the fruit beer category at the U.S. Beer Championship, and various Fair showings have also resulted in high honors.

Meanwhile, at the popular café, the beat goes on. Housed in a beautifully restored century-old wood frame building, the pub has developed a full menu of appetizers, soups, sandwiches and burgers, pizzas, salads and desserts. Specialties vary according to the season, but feature hearty favorites like Stout Beef Stew, made from the brewery's own Eight Ball Stout and organically raised beef, Lost Coast Vegetarian Chili, and Barbara's Bayou Prawns.

"Everything's fresh, and most of it's local," Groom says with justifiable pride. "Our coffee's freshly roasted at Humboldt Bay Coffee Company two blocks away. Our beef comes from the North Coast Co-Op which sells only Humboldt grass-fed beef. We even make our own root beer."

Augmenting the fresh/local concept, Groom has had local muralist Duane Flatmo design many of her labels. "Friends had already introduced us. Then I saw one of his posters and I thought, 'That's exactly how I think Mr. Downtown

Brown looks.' (Downtown Brown is the name of the brewery's award-winning brown ale.) So I called Duane and told him what I wanted, and he gave it to me. The Great White label was pretty much the same thing.

"With the Indica (IPA) label, Duane and I both talked to a number of India-born people to make certain that they wouldn't find the use of the Ganesh image offensive on a beer label. It's been pretty controversial in spite of our efforts, but I still like it.

"As far as the future is concerned, we're currently looking for a larger property, one where we can offer brewery tours, a restaurant and a gift shop. We're outgrowing our warehouse, and we're going to have to have more room.

"I love it that we hear from people thousands of miles away telling us how good our products are. I love it even more that some of them actually travel all the way to Eureka to see how our products are made.

"The distribution thing is a challenge because most towns have a small number of beer distributors, and the big breweries pretty much dictate what they do. But where we can get our products on the shelves, they sell."

Lost Coast's website asks, "What could be more fun than to get up every day and make beers you love and serve them to an appreciative public?"

Barbara Groom has done that, and continues to do it. Her answer might be, "Nothing. It doesn't get any better than this."

Meanwhile, fifteen miles south, in sunny Fortuna, Ted and Margaret Vivatson, like many people with day jobs, reached a point where they wanted a change. Ted, who had been home-brewing for years, said, "Let's open a micro-brewery." Margaret said, "What's that?"

His answer must have been convincing. In 1995, they opened Eel River Brewing Company, a business Ted Vivatson describes as "a benevolent dictatorship. It's that old Harry Truman thing: 'The buck stops here.' But all my brewers are involved in the process. A great staff makes it possible. I tell them what I want in terms of taste, in terms of bitterness, in terms of who I want it to appeal to, and they give it to me. Everybody gets to have input. Everybody's taste is different, but when it all comes together, it's a beautiful thing.

"I'm a Master Brewer. I train all my brewers and send them to school. There's a lot of science and math involved in the brew-making process, and the ones who can handle the science and math are the ones who stay on.

"I promote individualism and input. Allowing the staff to have input lets them take pride in their work. We're the most award-winning brewery in Humboldt County. When a beer wins a gold medal, and one of my brewers gets to say, 'That's *my* beer,' it's terrific."

He is so open to suggestion that when a patron asked why Eel River didn't make an organic beer, Vivatson decided to give it a try. At the time, the California Certified Organic Farmers had no guidelines for beer. Vivatson worked with them to create standards using the California Organic Foods Act of 1990 as a reference.

Eel River's Organic Amber Ale, the first California brew to be certified organic, returned from its trip to the California State Fair, in 2001, with a silver medal and some terrific press. Charlie Papazian, author of *The New Complete Joy of Home Brewing*, declared it "full flavored and wonderfully balanced."

Writing in *Playboy*, Benjamin Wachs said, "Beers brewed with organic ingredients tend to have a very bitter, biting flavor.... Organic Amber possesses the smooth, light flavor you typically associate with traditional ingredients, and its finish will leave you hungry for another."

Vivatson says, "I never expected to be in *Playboy*."

The brewery currently produces four gold medal winning organic beers: Amber Ale, Extra Pale Ale, IPA, and Porter. "Certification involves far more than just using certified organic ingredients," Vivatson explains. "It covers the processes we use, and a lot of record-keeping. You can buy a bottle of our certified organic beer anywhere and we can tell you where the ingredients in that bottle came from, when and how it was made."

And the records he must keep become even more involved. "At any given time we have twenty thousand to thirty thousand pounds of grain – which is mouse food – on hand. We can't put out poison; we have to use traps. I have a schematic diagram showing the location of every mousetrap in the building, and I record each time each trap is checked. It's a lot of work, but it's worthwhile. It keeps us on top of our game.

"We're taking the organic philosophy to a whole new level. We recently started raising our own Black Angus beef cattle. We feed them all the spent grain from the brewery and sweet alfalfa. No hormones. No antibiotics. The beef is out of this world. People ask what we use to season our hamburgers. We tell them, 'Nothing. We don't need to.'

"I love to cook. I've been working in kitchens most of my life. I started washing dishes when I was twelve years old, and I was making sauces by the time I was fifteen. Everything we do here is from scratch."

Indeed, Eel River has printed its company philosophy, the first credo of which states, "Great food takes longer. We prepare our food to order from scratch. It's not pre-measured, pre-cut or pre-cooked. This takes a while longer. But it will be worth it when it is served. So... sit down, relax, enjoy life. Have a beer!"

Vivatson takes obvious pride in the fact that Eel River is not a place where people come to drink to excess. Rather, it's a place for people to come and enjoy a good meal with a great beer. "I want to open people to new horizons for a better life. You should see this place on Sunday afternoons. It's packed with families who come in to eat after church.

"It was the first non-smoking bar in Humboldt County. People are welcome to sit outside in the beer garden and smoke. I'll even offer ashtrays." The beer garden is the largest of its kind on the North Coast with the capacity to seat up to one hundred people.

The pub itself features a thirty-foot-long bar fashioned exclusively from recovered historic redwoods and Douglas fir. The high white walls display framed photographic enlargements of local history, antique logging tools and occasional whimsy – a pair of well-worn lumberjack boots here, a graying union suit complete with drop seat there. Above it all, beneath the vaulted ceiling, large, full color plaques replicate the brewery's labels.

Vivatson surveys his kingdom and declares, "It's about love. All of our people love beer. The one thing I will *not* do is make bad beer."

NORTH COAST WAYS TO COOK WITH SPIRITS

Curley's guests love this one.

Curley's Lamb Shanks
   1/4 cup olive oil
   6 lamb shanks
   3 cups beef stock
   2 cups red wine
   kosher salt to taste
   3 bay leaves
   6 garlic cloves
   1 6-inch sprig of fresh rosemary
   2 teaspoons dried marjoram
   1 scant tablespoon peppercorns
   1 medium red onion, quartered

   Preheat oven to 325 degrees F.
   Heat olive oil in a large roasting pan. Add lamb shanks and sear them on all sides.
   Add the remaining ingredients. Cover with aluminum foil and bake until the meat is so tender it falls from the bones, approximately two hours.
   Taste for seasoning and serve.
   (6 servings)

Recipe courtesy of Curley Tait, Curley's Grill, Ferndale, California

Paul Clarke is a treasure trove of classic recipes for elegant, special occasions. This is an entree that he serves with App, or Fresh Grilled Duck Sausage (see Chapter 3) and a Three Beet Salad (See Chapter 4)

Tournedos Rossini
Fillet of Beef with Foie Gras and Perigord Truffle Sauce

    2 bunches of fresh spinach
    4 ounces butter, divided
    salt and pepper to taste
    4 slices bread, crusts trimmed and discarded
    4 tablespoons fresh parsley, finely chopped
    4 tournedos, well trimmed and shaped
    4 ounces foie gras (4 chicken livers, finely chopped, may be substituted)
    1 ounce garlic, chopped
    2 ounces shallots, chopped
    1 bay leaf
    1/8 teaspoon dried thyme
    1/8 teaspoon dried tarragon
    6 ounces red wine
    2 cups beef stock
    6 ounces truffle butter

Cook the spinach briefly in boiling water, drain and shock in ice water. Squeeze dry and chop.

In a sauté pan, melt one ounce of butter, add the spinach. Season with salt and pepper to taste, and keep warm until needed.

Trim the bread into octagonal croutons. In a sauté pan, melt one ounce of butter. Quickly fry the croutons to a crisp, golden brown. Remove from pan, spread with additional butter and sprinkle with chopped parsley. Reserve.

In a large sauté pan, melt the remaining butter over medium heat. Sauté the tournedos, somewhat slowly, turning as needed until rare, about five to six minutes per side. Remove, and keep warm.

Place the foie gras or livers in the pan and sauté until just cooked. Remove, and keep warm.

In the same pan, sauté the garlic and shallots over medium-low heat. When translucent, add bay, thyme and tarragon to the pan. Turn the heat to medium-high, add the wine, deglazing, and cook until liquid is reduced to 1/3 its original volume.

Pour in the beef stock and continue to reduce slowly until slightly thickened.

Stir in the truffle butter, then return the steaks to finish cooking.

To serve, arrange the croutons on a platter. Top with the reserved spinach. Place one steak on each, then top with the foie gras. Garnish with a little chopped parsley.

Taste the sauce for seasonings, adjust to taste.

Serve immediately, passing the sauce separately.

(4 servings)

Recipe courtesy of Chef Paul Clarke, The Groves at Riverbend, Myers Flat

If you're looking for a sure-fire way to feed a crowd, this recipe will do it. Of course, with a calculator (or a reasonably good head for math), the amounts can be scaled down to suit your needs. Either way, it's what one friend calls "a good goo."

Stout Beef Stew
> 6 cups flour
> 2 ounces paprika
> 2 ounces black pepper
> 2 ounces sage
> 2 ounces oregano
> 2 ounces whole thyme
> 4 ounces salt
> 1 cup olive oil
> 4 pounds onions, diced
> 1 quart Down Town Brown Beer
> 1 quart Eight Ball Stout Beer
> 8 quarts water or beef stock
> 3 pounds celery, thickly sliced
> ½ cup garlic, chopped
> 12 pounds stew meat, cubed
> 3 pounds carrots, thickly sliced
> 1 cup canola oil
> 4 pounds small red potatoes, scrubbed

Mix flour and seasonings and use the mixture to dredge the stew meat.

Blend the oils together and reserve 1/4 cup.

Heat remaining oil in a large stew pot.

Add the meat and half of the onions and sauté until the meat is browned and the onions caramelize.

 Add any remaining dredging flour along with the beers and water or stock. Cook for roughly 45minutes.

Meanwhile, in a separate pan, sauté the remaining onions, celery and garlic in reserved oil.

Add to the meat mixture.

Add carrots and potatoes. Bring to boil, then reduce heat and simmer 45 minutes to an hour, until carrots and potatoes are done.

(24 generous servings)

Recipe courtesy of Barbara Groom, Lost Coast Brewery and Café, Eureka

This is another of the Lost Coast's specialties. The quantity is smaller, but the taste is every bit as terrific.

Barbara's Prawns
   2 dozen large shrimp with heads and shells (about 1 pound)
   cold water to rinse
   1 teaspoon paprika
   1 teaspoon black pepper
   ½ teaspoon salt
   ½ teaspoon crushed red pepper
   ½ teaspoon dried thyme leaves
   ½ teaspoon crushed dried rosemary
   1/4 teaspoon dried oregano
   1/4 pound (1 stick) plus 5 tablespoons butter
   1 ½ teaspoon minced garlic
   ½ cup Down Town Brown Ale

   Rinse the shrimp in cold water. Drain thoroughly and set aside.
   In a small bowl, combine seasonings, mixing well.
   In a large skillet over high heat, combine one stick of butter, garlic and seasonings.
   When butter has melted, add the shrimp. Cook for 2 minutes, shaking the pan in a back and forth motion.
   Add the remaining butter and continue cooking in the same manner for 2 minutes more.
   Add the ale and cook one additional minute.
   Remove from heat, and serve with chunks of bread.
   (4 first course servings)

Recipe courtesy of Barbara Groom, Lost Coast Brewery and Café, Eureka

Margaret Haegart has cooked so long and so well that it's instinctive. She allowed me to shadow her, take notes and ask questions as she prepared these scrumptious potatoes for breakfast at the Lost Whale Inn. They would work equally well as a side dish for any meal.

Potatoes from The Lost Whale

    4 tablespoons butter
    4 cups potatoes, peeled and diced
    1 leek, cleaned and trimmed, white and light green parts only,
        thinly sliced
    seasoning salt (Margaret uses Montreal Chicken Seasoning)
        and pepper to taste
    1 cup white wine

Heat a large skillet over medium heat and add butter. When it has melted, add the diced potatoes and sliced leeks, coating well with the melted butter.

Sprinkle with seasonings.

Cook 15 minutes, shaking the pan and stirring the contents frequently.

Pour the cup of white wine over the potatoes and continue cooking until all the liquid is absorbed.

Test for doneness and serve.

(8 servings) (Expect requests for seconds)

Recipe courtesy of Chef Margaret Haegert, The Lost Whale Bed and Breakfast Inn, Trinidad

I love it when things I might never have imagined merge into something which tastes both intriguing and wonderful. This sauce, intended for asparagus, is a perfect example. Mike Vitiello adds that if you cannot find almond paste, you can make your own. Just finely grind 1 cup of blanched almonds with 1/4 cup brown sugar and a dash of almond extract.

Almond-Orange Cream Sauce

   1 tablespoon clarified butter
   1/4 teaspoon salt
   ½ teaspoon freshly ground white pepper
   2 tablespoons minced shallot
   1/4 cup almond paste
   1/4 cup white wine
   ½ cup orange juice
   2 cups heavy cream

In a medium sauté pan over medium heat, melt the butter. Add salt, pepper and minced shallots.

When shallots begin to turn golden in color, add the almond paste and white wine. Stirring frequently, let the wine reduce to 1/3 the original volume.

Add the orange juice. Raise the heat to bring the sauce to a boil and boil for two minutes.

Add the cream. Return the sauce to a boil, then lower heat so that mixture just simmers. Continue cooking 5 minutes.

Serve over freshly steamed or roasted asparagus.

(will dress 4 servings)

Recipe courtesy of Chef Mike Vitiello, Hurricane Kate's, Old Town, Eureka

Poached pears are wonderful, but adding a warm semi-sweet chocolate sauce sets them apart – somewhere around the realm of rapturous.

Pears Poached in Sauterne with Warm Chocolate Sauce

For the Pears:
  1 bottle good quality Sauterne
  1 cup sugar
  1 vanilla bean, split in half lengthwise
  3 anise stars
  4 firm pears

In a deep stainless steel sauce pan, combine the wine, sugar and spices, and bring to a boil.

Meanwhile, peel pears, leaving stems intact. Immerse pears in boiling liquid, making sure they are totally submerged. Add more wine if necessary.

Return to a boil, then reduce heat and simmer, covered, until pears are tender, but not mushy (1 to 2 hours, depending on the size of the pears).

Remove from heat and refrigerate overnight in the poaching liquid.

When ready to serve, scoop out the pears and drain.

Proceed with the sauce.

For the Sauce:
  10 ounces excellent quality semi-sweet chocolate
  3/4 cups heavy cream

Chop the chocolate and place in a small heat-proof bowl.

In a small saucepan, bring the cream to a boil.

Pour cream over the chocolate and stir until chocolate is completely melted, and the mixture is smooth and shiny. Pour, immediately, over pears and serve.

  (4 servings)

Recipe courtesy of Chef Alex Begovic, Personal Caterer, Eureka

The recent interest in chevre has opened all kinds of dining doors, and here in Humboldt County, we're blessed to have some of the best in the world available to us. This recipe uses chevre in a dessert form, but Mary Keehn suggests that the basic recipe could serve equally well as a cake filling, a topping for blintzes or a dressing for a fresh fruit salad.

Brandy Crème Dessert

    1 pound Fromage Blanc (ideally from Cypress Grove Chevre)
    ½ cup whipped cream
    1/4 cup powdered sugar
    2 tablespoons brandy
    2 cups warmed raspberries or warmed blackberries

Whip the goat cheese, whipped cream, powdered sugar and brandy together in a food processor with a whip attachment.

Ladle, by spoonfuls, into parfait glasses, adding warm berries between layers and using the berries to finish the presentation.

Serve immediately.

(4 servings)

Recipe courtesy Mary Keehn, proprietor, Cypress Grove Chevre, McKinleyville

Another of Chef Alex Begovic's phenomenal creations. He truly has a flair for turning traditional French food concepts into explosions of taste and texture.

**Rum-Flambéed Bananas folded into Crepes
with Coconut Cream Sauce**

Have all ingredients at room temperature.

Batter for crepes: Crepes may be made up to a day ahead of time and stored between sheets of parchment.
   3 whole eggs
   1 ½ cup of milk
   1 cup flour
   ½ tablespoon sugar
   ½ tablespoon salt
   2 tablespoons melted butter

In medium bowl, beat eggs until smooth.
Add the milk and stir until well-blended.
Whisk in the flour, sugar and salt. Mix thoroughly and pour mixture through a fine mesh sieve.
Add melted butter and let batter rest at room temperature one hour.
When ready to make crepes, mix batter until evenly smooth.
Using a ladle, spoon about one ounce of batter into a lightly buttered, small, non-stick pan over medium-low heat until lightly browned.
Remove to parchment and continue making crepes until all batter is used.

For the Coconut Sauce:
 1 cup sweetened condensed milk (scrape can to remove entire contents)
 2 cups coconut milk
 1 vanilla bean, split lengthwise, making sure the seeds are exposed

 In a small, non-aluminum saucepan, mix all ingredients.
 Over medium heat, bring to a simmer, stirring often with a wooden spoon. Lower heat and let simmer for 10 to 15 minutes, being careful not to caramelize. (If brown bits begin to form, press through a fine sieve.)

For the Banana Filling:
 4 firm (less than ripe bananas)
 4 tablespoons butter (½ stick)
 1/4 cup brown sugar
 1/4 cup rum
 fresh mangoes, strawberries, etc.
 fresh mint for garnish

 In a large NON-STICK sauté pan, over medium heat, melt butter.
 Slice bananas and add.
 Add sugar and cook until sugar is golden and almost caramelized, stirring often.
 Pour rum into pan and flambé.
 Spoon filling into crepes.
 Fold crepes over and drizzle with coconut sauce.
 Finish with fresh fruit such as mangoes, strawberries, etc. and garnish with mint sprigs.
 (4 servings)

Recipe courtesy Chef Alex Begovic, Personal Caterer, Eureka

Hurricane Kate is the undisputed queen of the deliciously unexpected and the unexpectedly delicious. Witness the following recipe which she insists you read all the way through before attempting to duplicate:

Ginger Stout Cake
 6 1/4 cups all-purpose flour
 1 tablespoon baking soda
 2 tablespoons baking powder
 3 tablespoons ground ginger
 2 tablespoons cinnamon, ground
 2 teaspoons ground white pepper
 1 teaspoon cloves, ground
 1 teaspoon Kosher salt
 1 pound softened (NOT melted!) butter
 2 cups light brown sugar
 5 eggs
 2 ½ cups molasses
 2 ½ cups Oatmeal Stout, flat, at room temperature

Preheat oven to 350 degrees F.

Sift the flour, soda, baking powder, ginger, cinnamon, white pepper, cloves and Kosher salt together in a large mixing bowl.

In the bowl of a mixer fitted with a wire whip combine butter and brown sugar. Beat on high speed until very light and fluffy, at least three minutes.

Add the eggs, one at a time, beating on high after each addition. Beat for one more minute.

Add molasses and Stout. Mix until just combined. The batter will be lumpy and curdled-looking.

Add this batter to the dry ingredients all at once.

Combine thoroughly using a wire whip.

Transfer to a 14"x 14"pan that has been greased and floured.

Bake at 350 degrees F for 30 minutes.

Rotate and bake 20 minutes more.

Cool on a wire rack. Cut and serve.
DO NOT REFRIGERATE EVER!!
(As many as 49 servings, depending on size)

At Hurricane Kate's they serve this topped with ice cream – either white chocolate or ginger – both produced at Bon Boniere, a confectionery right around the corner. It's out of this world.

Recipe courtesy of Kate Chadwick, Hurricane Kate's, Old Town Eureka

Tofu in Smoker, Tofu Shop   © *Matthew Filar*

CHAPTER SEVEN

FOOD PRODUCERS

Humboldt County draws creative people from all over the world. Some come to attend the University and never leave. Others crave an environment in which natural beauty feeds their artistic spirits. Still others look for a lifestyle that affords time to follow their bliss while providing consistent cultural stimuli. California's North Coast offers all this and more.

Often there's a trade-off involved. There are no elegant, multi-storied department stores with high-end designer fashions. There are no major corporations paying executives six-figure salaries. There are no major league athletic teams playing in arenas that seat tens of thousands of fans. If these things matter greatly to you, you would not want to live in Humboldt County, although you might certainly enjoy visiting there.

There are, however museums, art galleries, theater companies and venues featuring remarkably good live music. There are painters, photographers, potters, sculptors and fine furniture craftspeople whose work you may have admired in museums near you. There are authors whose books you may read to your children at bedtime; jewelry makers whose designs you may already own and treasure; chefs whose menus may have delighted you in restaurants around the world. And there are food producers packaging products from seafood to sauces, tofu to fine Belgian chocolate, sought out by gourmets from coast to coast.

Like her sister Deborah, Patty Lazio Callison grew up in the market section of the family's seafood restaurant. "I used to go into the back and carry out fish that were bigger than I was," she says, laughing at the recollection. "I was great with the fish, but I was scared of the cash register."

Today the restaurant is gone, but the Lazios still market premium, line-caught albacore using the family recipe that has been handed down for four generations. And Patty, at the helm of their retail operation has long since recovered from her fear. If your idea of canned tuna is the flavorless, texture less pap found on most supermarket shelves, you owe it to yourself to try "the real thing." But hold onto your hat. Cans with the Lazio label offer you an entirely different experience.

"We have strict standards," she explains. "All the tuna we use is top grade albacore, which is the only kind that can be labeled 'solid-pack white' or 'chunk white.' We process only in small batches so that we can control the quality. And our workers know what they're doing. So often large companies will hire the cheapest labor they can find to keep the costs down. Lazio has never worked that way. Our product has our name on it. It has to be good.

"And it's all albacore. We don't use any hydrolyzed protein or any tuna 'flakes.' With many larger brands the hydrolyzed protein content can run as high as eighteen percent, and as much as seventeen percent may be 'flake.' That can add up to thirty-five percent filler in a can. The difference is huge."

And noticeable. Linda Eckhardt's *Great Food Catalog,* an IACP Julia Child Award-winning compendium of food products to mail order throughout the United States, has become a bible for the pickiest cooks. In the book Eckhardt tells the world, "The first time I opened one of these cans, I could hardly recognize the stuff....It looked like tuna I'd poached."

The online Rebecca's Review calls it "the best tuna on the market," and "a real winner."

The Washington Post says, "This is no ordinary tuna. Lazio sells some of the best albacore we've tasted."

New York Times writer John Leland relates that no less a luminary in the food world than Julia Child invited him to lunch at her home, promising him a tuna sandwich. She served him leftover lobster instead, but as he was leaving she gave him a can of Lazio albacore to make good her word. Child, as a matter of policy, makes no personal endorsements, but word has leaked out that she's on Lazio's mail order list.

While the albacore remains their biggest seller, Lazio now offers other delicacies in season. Smoked sturgeon, Italian-style salmon and Dungeness crab all carry the Lazio label when available, and all measure up to the family's high standards.

The little girl with the big fish is still in the Eureka business, bigger and better than ever.

Not far from the Lazio outlet, Marie Wilkins does her own thing with a style all her own. She was seven years old when her grandmother began teaching her to cook. "She taught me right," she says, a bright smile spreading across her entire face. "I did it her way, or I didn't eat. You know what I'm saying?"

The whole family pulled together to put meals on the table. "We didn't waste anything. We'd even rinse out the containers with a little bit of water to make sure we got every last bit. And meat was a luxury. We learned to make do with all kinds of things. But it always tasted real good."

In Opelousas, Louisiana, the Creole cultural tradition inspired full-flavored food. When her grandmother, for health reasons, moved the family to Los Angeles, that tradition went with them.

As an adult, Marie worked in films as a dancer. But when her daughter Desiree was born she opened a catering business from her Topanga Canyon home in order to be a full time mother. The Creole tradition, her grandmother's lessons, and her own deep love of cooking combined to bring her enormous success.

She soon found herself in demand by the film studios. "A lot of directors didn't want condiments and sauces that came out of cans, so I began experimenting with things I thought they'd like. One director in particular was very fond of ham, so I made up a mustard sauce for him. I was stirring it with a wooden spoon that had a skinny little handle, and the sauce was so thick that the handle broke. So I whipped out my kitchen gloves and went to mixing it with my hands.

"My daughter came into the kitchen, and I held up my hands. They had all this mustard sauce stuck to them, and I said, 'Desiree, I love this sauce, but it's so sticky.' She said, 'That's what you should call it, Mama: Sticky Love Sauce.'

"My friend Taj Mahal (the jazz musician) was living at our house at the time. He knew that my full name was Marie Janisse, and he started calling me "Sweet Mama Janisse.' He even wrote a song by that name, and they still play it on the radio. So that's how 'Sweet Mama Janisse's Sticky Love Sauce' got its name.

"Now it's in the Mount Horeb Mustard Museum in Mount Horeb, Wisconsin. And we took it to the World Mustard Festival in the Napa Valley. There were huge mustard companies there. Some of them had twenty or thirty different kinds of mustard. I walked in with one little tiny jar of mustard, and it won a bronze medal. I was so proud!"

The mustard is just one of a line of products she now markets under the Sweet Mama Janisse label. Others include a chili pepper paste, a hot soy-gin sauce, a barbecue sauce she calls "Soy-Q" and her "Mint to Love" sauce. She also has a refrigerated spread she's named "Sweet Mama Janisse's Spread Me Please."

When the pace in Los Angeles became overwhelming, Marie moved her catering business and product line to Eureka. Now, in a Victorian residence right on US 101, in a busy downtown area, she also runs Bless My Soul Café.

Out front, in stark contrast to the surrounding concrete commercial structures, gardens splashed with blooms in vibrant colors tell us that something beyond the ordinary reigns inside. And if brightness and vibrancy appeal to diners, they won't go away disappointed.

Still drawing on the Creole tradition, Marie has designed a menu to satisfy all the senses. Entrees like Jambalaya, Caribbean Jerk Chicken and Fried Catfish; a la carte items and appetizers including Hush Puppies, Broiled Bayou Shrimp, Louisiana Hot Links, and Dirty Rice, all find a place on the menu. And that Soul Food classic, Sweet Potato Pie, tops the list of desserts.

There's also a wine list, a choice of beers, even grape Kool Aid. Really. Diners, of course, can request any of her sauces and condiments to accompany the meal. If you can't make it to Bless My Soul, you can find Marie online. How can you resist something called "Sweet Mama Janisse's Sticky Love Sauce"?

Less than a mile from Bless My Soul, in the heart of Eureka's Old Town, Jacques Holten makes Sjaak's Fine Belgian Chocolates. Just entering the shop is a heady experience. The aroma moves directly from the nose to the brain, mellowing the most tense of patrons. The visual array of truffles, nut clusters, bars and specialty shapes mounts a friendly assault on the senses as well.

When he was thirteen years old, Jacques Holten entered an apprenticeship at the Voorhout Institute of Pastry and Confectionary in his home town of Venlo, Holland. Six years of intensive training earned him a Masters degree in baking and confections. Then he went to work setting up and running bakeries and chocolate shops from Germany to Istanbul to Costa del Sol.

In Spain he met his wife Pam, a Spanish major from Eureka, who was studying in Granada. Ultimately they moved to her home town where he opened Sjaak's European Bake Shop. As both his family and his business grew, however, the long hours that bakeries demand increasingly impinged on his home life. In 1977, he sold out and went to work for Safeway.

His strong entrepreneurial spirit remained, however, and in 1985 he opened Sjaak's Fine Belgian Chocolates in the heart of Eureka's Old Town. Today he and his staff create and sell an ever-growing variety of endorphin-producing confections according to the highest European and American standards.

"We use three major processes," he explains. "We make our own ganaches, or soft centers: rich butter cream flavored with espresso, fruits and nut butters. We shape and hand-dip them. The work must be done very quickly, because they melt at body temperature.

"'Enrobed' items use a slower method. Centers are firmer – nuts, ginger or orange slices pass through a machine that coats them with melted chocolate. This produces a smoother, shinier finish than you get with hand-dipped pieces.

"In the third process, we use poly-carbon molds which are filled with melted chocolate and then quickly emptied. This leaves a thin chocolate shell lining the mold. We fill the shell with very soft centers and then top them with more chocolate. The molded chocolates are the smoothest and shiniest of all."

Holten uses custom molds to offer replicas of local images like crabs and banana slugs. Customers can even purchase small chocolate versions of The Carson Mansion, said to be the most photographed Victorian home in North America, and a focal point for Old Town visitors. Additionally, hand-wrapped pieces in sparkling red, green or gold foil brighten the showroom, as do his specially designed gift boxes.

If customers can tear their eyes from the aforementioned intoxicating array of choices, they can watch through a large showroom window as employees in the factory create the confections. The easy, good-natured interaction indicates that his workers are as overtaken as visitors by the sensory appeal, and Holten appears to enjoy it as much as anyone. Does he ever tire of it? "Of course there are days when it would be nice to stay in bed. But tire of it? Never. I love what I do."

Holten attributes the success of his business to two basic principles. "We never compromise on the quality of our ingredients," he declares. "We use no margarines or hydrogenated oils, no artificial flavors. Our chocolate is made from high-grade cacao beans, sugar, milk powder and, sometimes, a little pure vanilla. We roast our own nuts, slowly, to bring out the full flavor, and we make our own nut butters. We use some domestic chocolate, but about seventy percent of it comes from Belgium."

Freshness is the second factor. "We're small, so our products never end up stored in warehouses. They move right from the factory into the showroom to the customer. Storing isn't bad for chocolate.... It doesn't make chocolate 'spoil,' but oxidation begins immediately, and before long the aroma and flavor begin to fade. When you put on cologne, the same thing happens. At first the fragrance is apparent, but after several hours, it disappears. The cologne hasn't gone bad. It's just undergone oxidation."

Beginning in 2004, Holten has offered a line of organic chocolate. The business has met the criteria for certification, and he looks forward to further expansion. But, as always, the emphasis will remain on quality ingredients and freshness.

The cacao beans, which anthropologists think have been considered a delicacy for at least two millennia, continue to delight consumers as creative processors like Jacques Holten invent new ways to enjoy them. The world is different from the traditions that spawned Sjaak's Fine Belgian Chocolates. But the new technology allows anyone, anytime, to sample his Old World creations. You can order them on line – you just can't smell the shop that way.

Neighboring Arcata, like the rest of Humboldt County, is rife with idiosyncrasies. It's a college town, but not your traditional "halls of ivy" college town. Rather, in many ways it resembles a miniature version of Berkeley, home of free thought and ethnic diversity.

Not the least (or the least controversial) of its quirks is its moratorium on fast food franchises. You won't find a Burger King in Arcata. Or Krispy Kreme Donuts. Or Taco Bell. So what's a struggling college student to grab and eat between classes?

One option might be an avocado wasabi wrap from Pacific Rim Noodle House – one option of many. The tiny take-out house, under a gingko tree, within walking distance of the Plaza, has put together a simple menu of complex flavors typical of spots along the opposite side of the Pacific Rim. Rice bowls, noodle bowls, sushi wraps and daily specials give "fast food" a new and much welcomed lease on life.

The business began in 1994, when Catlin Conlin came home to Arcata and told her mother, Carol Davis, "I need a job."

"I needed one too," says Davis recalling the event. "I'd done a lot of different things over the years when the children were growing up, but I was really ready to find something of my own. So we decided to join forces in something. We just weren't exactly sure what that something would be."

They shared a love of food, so that seemed a natural choice, but the pair needed to find a focus. They attended a natural food trade show in Los Angeles, and followed that with a fancy food trade show in San Francisco. "In the car coming home, Catlin and I looked at each other and said, simultaneously, 'Noodle House,' and it all began to come together.

"Catlin had a friend who came in to do sushi. Then an American Field Service teacher from Thailand brought us all her family's recipes. They owned Thai restaurants all over, even in Frankfurt, Germany. So that was a huge help.

"Catlin and I went down to the California Culinary Institute in San Francisco and took classes in Chinese and Korean cuisines, and one specifically on Pacific Rim cuisine. We really packed a lot into it. And the timing was good. People were just beginning to learn about the wonderful foods from that part of the world."

Davis feels that she and her daughter make a good team. "Catlin is detail-oriented. She loves to perfect what we're doing here. I'm more creative. I love to experiment and try new combinations. But we're both passionate about food and cooking."

It was Catlin who developed their first sauce, Creamy Wasabi. "We were serving rice, noodles and vegetables," Davis reflects, "but we needed something wonderful to put on them. The sauce was smooth and creamy, so the texture didn't interfere with the food, but the wasabi gave it a real kick."

Not to be outdone, Davis came up with their Island Ginger Orange Sauce. And so they progressed to the point where, as of this writing, they have a total of six sauces on the market, each strikingly different from the others, all of them zesty and flavorful.

"Distribution has been a struggle," Davis admits. "It's a tough area when you're a small company. We've had three co-packers in seven years. Right now we're working with an organization in Cotati, near Santa Rosa. They're close enough to keep in contact and know what's going on. And we have a Canadian distributor who picks up the product and has put it on a lot of shelves. We ran across it in British Columbia."

For Davis, it's a joy to be able to be doing what she loves, but there are altruistic perks, too. "I feel like I'm offering working mothers an alternative to the hot dogs, hamburgers and pizza they've been limited to for so long." And she likes the fact that the products they use in the noodle house, from tofu to fresh vegetables, are all locally produced. "It's a great way to be able to give something back to the community."

The tofu she uses is produced nearby at The Tofu Shop.

In Colorado, in 1977, Matthew Schmit helped to put together a food co-op focused on local products. Having become a vegetarian two years earlier, he was disappointed by the lack of meatless choices on most menus at the time. So he was excited when he met a couple who had read *The Book of Tofu* and taught themselves to make the soybean curd.

"When I finished my work day as manager of the co-op, I'd go over to their place and work from ten at night until six the next morning, turning out about twelve pounds of tofu an evening. We'd package the blocks in baggies, wrap a twist tie around them and sell them at the co-op."

Schmit and a friend rented a shop space, set up a kitchen, developed some recipes and began a take-out restaurant. At the same time, they distributed their products on a wholesale basis across the western Colorado slope. His partner dropped out somewhere along the way, and Schmit continued the operation on his own. Understandably, by 1979, he had burned out.

"My sister was living here in Humboldt County, and I came out here, I suppose, to reinvent myself. I worked for awhile as a carpenter's assistant, but it was a tough job market. Then I cooked at The Sprouted Seed, which is now Wild Flower Bakery.

"Tofu was here. People in Arcata were buying it, and cooking with it. A shop space came up for rent, and a friend and I took it. In 1980, we opened a tofu shop modeled after the neighborhood tofu shops in Japan.

"We stayed there until the Arcata Economic Development Council opened Food Works, a co-operative venture for specialty food producers. It was a tremendous idea, way ahead of its time. But ultimately I realized it wasn't going to fly.

"There was an odd-shaped lot nearby that carried a very reasonable price tag. We were able to get local funding, so we bought it and built our own plant. The Tofu Shop opened there in January, 2001."

Schmit now employs a staff of twenty-three to produce his certified organic soy products. They use dried whole organic soybeans that they soak overnight in filtered water to soften. Next they grind the beans into a paste, and cook it in boiling water. Then they strain the paste, separating the soy milk from the soybean pulp.

Using magnesium chloride, they curdle the soy milk, ladle the curds into boxes, and press the curds into shape. Once the curd sets, they cut it into blocks which they pack into plastic containers. The entire process is done by hand using open cauldrons in the Japanese tradition.

Schmit has expanded his line to twenty-three products. In addition to unflavored blocks, The Tofu Shop offers chocolate, ginger, vanilla and unflavored soy milk, three kinds of smoked tofu, four varieties of baked tofu, and five different spreads. Most recently, they've added chorizo-spiced, tandoori-spiced and Thai-spiced tofus.

He respects and treasures his connection to the community. "We get called on a lot for donations to community organizations and fund raisers. We never say no." In addition, he has set up a system whereby 99.7 percent of the shop's waste is recycled. Soybean pulp, one hundred twenty tons of it each year, goes to local ranchers as livestock feed. Everything else that can be accepted at the local recycling center is sorted and taken there. Schmit expresses both admiration and appreciation for a community network where this is an option. "We discard only one thirty-two gallon can of trash each week," he says.

California Waste Reduction Awards Program honored The Tofu Shop in 2002 for being one of the state's top ten leaders in waste reduction. "What feels really good," Schmit says, "is that we were already doing that. We didn't have to change our system to win.

"I'm happy right now. I know growth is necessary in business. I want to be able to provide a good living for a core group of employees, and to be able to make the job attractive for part-time people. But I also want to maintain our identity as a local company.

"We're just beginning to expand our distribution. We're now in organic and health food stores in southern Oregon and the San Francisco Bay Area. Realistically, that's good, but I'm taking it one day at a time."

About four miles east, in Blue Lake, Tomaso' s Specialty Foods and Distribution has its own story.

One day, at the age of five, Tom Pagano wanted breakfast. His mother had gone, briefly, to visit neighbors in another unit of their New Jersey apartment building. But that didn't deter the resourceful boy. He climbed up on the stove and fried an egg himself.

He's been cooking ever since.

He might tell you he considers it the most natural thing in the world. After all, he's Italian. "For Italians," he says, "food and family are the most important things in life – and probably in that order," he adds with a broad smile.

"My Grandma Pauline," he continues, "made everything from scratch. Bread, pasta, sauces, all of it. And she'd only use the best, the freshest ingredients." It's no wonder food and cooking hold a place in his heart.

Pagano discovered Humboldt County in 1971 at the age of twenty-three. The following year he opened his first restaurant, Tomaso's Tomato Pies in Old

Town Eureka. After eight successful years, he sold the business, but retained rights to the name.

In the 1980's he opened and sold another restaurant, and worked as chef at various establishments including the Ingomar Club, an exclusive social group housed in the famed Carson Mansion. He finished the decade as executive chef at Abruzzi and the Plaza Grill in Arcata.

For several years he had spent his weekends in the kitchen of his Trinidad apartment. He would make up batches of his family's marinara sauce, pack it into glass jars and sell them through a couple of grocery stores in the area. But before long, he couldn't keep up with the orders. In an apartment, two days a week, he could only make two and a half cases at a time. But it was the food he loved to make, so he followed his heart. As 1990 dawned, Pagano's full time and energy went into Tomaso's Specialty Foods. And it has paid off in steady growth.

Today he has a total of twenty-five sauces and condiments that he markets. The marinara is still his favorite, "because it's so versatile." But he now offers variations: Spicy Eggplant; Fresh Mushroom and Artichoke; Black Olive, Fresh Basil and Garlic; several pestos; an Alfredo and a Puttanesca.

The labels all pay tribute to his Grandma Pauline, and the care and attention to detail she demanded as well as her emphasis on the freshest ingredients. Pagano proclaims that Tomaso's is "the small company with the big Italian flavor," and he's absolutely right. Athough he's moved from his apartment kitchen to quarters in an industrial park in Blue Lake, he keeps his output to a level he can monitor and guarantee the quality.

In addition to doing his own distributing, Pagano has taken on the distribution of other locally produced products. "There seemed to be a need for it," he says with a humility that discounts the role he has played in the success of others in Humboldt's food industry.

Now Tomaso's Specialty Foods and Distribution reaps the same success he's always enjoyed. He credits Grandma Pauline. The rest of us just get to enjoy.

Mangia!

NORTH COAST WAYS TO USE LOCAL PRODUCTS

This salad can be served either hot or cold. It goes together very quickly, so it's important to have all of the ingredients assembled before you begin. Leftovers make a refreshing change in a lunch box, too.

Asian Albacore-Noodle Salad
  8 ounces Japanese Soba Noodles
  1/4 cup peanut oil
  3 tablespoons Soy sauce
  3 tablespoons rice wine vinegar
  1 tablespoon lime juice
  1 tablespoon brown sugar
  1 egg
  1 7-ounce can Lazio Gourmet Albacore in water, drained and flaked
  3 cloves garlic, minced
  2 tablespoons grated fresh ginger
  1/4 cup sliced green onion, green and white parts
  1/4 cup very finely shredded carrot
  1/4 cup very finely shredded cabbage
  1/4 cup finely chopped cilantro

Cook noodles in boiling water according to package directions. Drain, and place into a mixing bowl. Dress with 2 to 3 tablespoons of the peanut oil. Toss to make sure strands are evenly coated. Set aside.

In a cup, mix Soy sauce, rice wine vinegar, lime juice and brown sugar. Mix until brown sugar completely dissolves. Set aside.

In a small bowl, beat the egg. Add albacore and stir to thoroughly coat the fish.

Heat a large sauté pan or wok over high heat. Add the remaining peanut oil and swirl the pan to coat. Pour in the albacore-egg mixture. Stir-fry quickly one minute. Push the mixture to the sides of the pan.

Add the garlic and ginger. Stir-fry thirty seconds, then push into albacore-egg mix.

Add green onions, carrots, and cabbage, one at a time, stir-frying each addition briefly.

Add the reserved noodles and cook, stirring together all the ingredients in the pan, five minutes.

Pour in the reserved Soy sauce mixture. Cook, stirring, five more minutes.

Place in a serving bowl, and garnish with cilantro.

(2 main course or 4 salad servings)

This is an up-dated version of a comfort-food stand-by. It's colorful, flavorful and filled with things that are good for you.

Albacore-Stuffed Peppers
4 medium red bell peppers
1 tablespoon olive oil
½ cup finely chopped shallots
2 cloves garlic, minced
2 cups chopped mushrooms
2/3 cup chopped parsley
1/4 cup slivered almonds, lightly toasted
1/4 cup dry white wine
1 tablespoon ground marjoram
1 ½ cups hot cooked rice
2 7-ounce cans Lazio Gourmet Albacore in water, flaked
1 cup tomato juice
1/4 cup sliced ripe olives
salt and pepper to taste
4 tablespoons freshly grated Parmesan cheese

Preheat oven to 350 degrees F.
Cut tops from peppers. Carefully remove and discard seeds and membranes. Drop peppers in boiling water and cook eight minutes. Drain and reserve.
Heat a large skillet over medium-high heat. Add oil and swirl pan to coat.
Sauté shallots two minutes. Add garlic and sauté one minute.
Add mushrooms and sauté four minutes.
Add parsley, almonds, wine, marjoram, rice, albacore, tomato juice, olives, salt and pepper. Sauté three minutes.
Pack mixture into reserved bell peppers. Top each pepper with one tablespoon cheese.
Place peppers in a 9" square baking dish and bake fifteen minutes. Serve at once.
(4 servings)

Marie takes advantage of Farmers Market offerings to pull this colorful dish together. The full spectrum of color makes a spectacular presentation.

Tofu Creole
oil of your choice for sautéing
½ red bell pepper, sliced
½ yellow bell pepper, sliced
½ green bell pepper, sliced
½ orange bell pepper, sliced
1//2 red onion, sliced
2 - 3 ribs celery, sliced
3 large cloves garlic, sliced
2 fresh tomatoes, cut into wedges
1 tablespoon dried thyme
1 tablespoon dried marjoram
1 tablespoon granulated garlic
1 pound The Tofu Shop extra-firm tofu, drained and cubed
6 jalapeno peppers, stemmed and seeded (you may substitute serranos)
6 cloves fresh garlic
2 cups lemon juice
kosher salt to taste

In a large Dutch Oven, over medium high heat, sauté bell peppers, onion and celery five to six minutes.

Add garlic and tomatoes and sauté two minutes more. Add marjoram, thyme and granulated garlic, stirring to blend.

Add tofu, stirring well. Reduce heat to low.

In a blender, process peppers, garlic, lemon juice and kosher salt into pure liquid. Add to the mixture, a bit at a time, tasting, until it's to your liking.

(4 generous servings)

Recipe courtesy Marie Wilkins, Sweet Mama Janisse Products and Bless My Soul Café, Eureka

Traditionally, you might use Tomaso's Marinara sauce and mozzarella on a pre-baked pizza crust – and it would be good. But for a fresher version, try it this way.

Updated Pizza
  2 12-inch pre-baked thin pizza crusts
  1 7-ounce container Tomaso's fresh basil and garlic pesto suce
  12 mushroom caps, thinly sliced
  6 sun-dried tomatoes, oil-packed, drained and chopped
  1 jar marinated artichoke heats, drained and cut, lengthwise, into eighths
  8 ounces crumbled Feta cheese

Preheat oven to 450 degrees F.
Spread pesto equally on crusts
Arrange mushroom slices, tomato bits and artichoke slices in pesto.
Sprinkle crumbled Feta cheese over all.
Bake eight to ten minutes, until crusts are nicely browned and cheese melts.
Slice each pizza into six wedges and serve hot.
(as many as 12 slices)

This is a hearty dish, great for cold winter evenings. Tom urges the use of whole milk cheeses (ricotta and mozzarella) for maximum flavor. If your supermarket doesn't stock them, try an Italian market. If you use aluminum foil to cover the casserole, take care that it does not come in contact with the food.

Baked Ziti

1 pound ziti dry pasta
2 jars Tomaso's Fresh Basil and Garlic Marinara Sauce
2 15-ounce containers ricotta cheese
1 pound shredded mozzarella
½ cup grated Parmesan or Romano cheese
1 large bunch Italian flat leaf parsley, leaves only, chopped
1 cup heavy cream
½ teaspoon salt
½ teaspoon pepper

Preheat oven to 350 degrees F.

Fill a large pot with water. Bring to a boil and add the pasta, cooking according to package directions. Drain and rinse under cold water. Set aside.

In a large bowl, mix half a jar of marinara sauce, all of the ricotta, three-fourths of the mozzarella, the Parmesan, parsley, cream, salt and pepper.

When well-blended, add the reserved pasta, folding it in gently.

Oil a 13"x9"x2" glass or enamel baking dish. Pour in the remaining half-jar of sauce, spreading it over entire bottom of the pan.

Add the pasta-cheese mixture, spreading it evenly.

Pour the remaining jar of marinara sauce evenly over the casserole.

Sprinkle with the remaining mozzarella.

Cover and bake forty to forty-five minutes.

(6 servings)

Recipe courtesy of Tom Pagano. Tomaso's Specialty Foods, Blue Lake

The great thing about bottled sauces is that they not only enhance flavor, but they can speed preparation time. This recipe is a classic example.

Island Ginger Orange Tropical Baked Fish

2 pounds white fish (such as sole, halibut or cod)
½ cup Pacific Rim Noodle House Island Ginger Orange Sauce

Preheat oven to 400 degrees F.
Wrap fish and sauce in foil, folding edges twice to seal well.
Bake ten to fifteen minutes depending on the thickness of the fish. It should flake easily with a fork. Do not over-bake. Serve hot.
(6 servings)

Recipe courtesy of Carol Davis, Pacific Rim Noodle House, Arcata

This is another amazingly quick dish. It works as a side, or served over rice or soba noodles as a main dish.

Fresh Mushrooms and Bok Choy with Black Bean Sauce
2 bunches bok choy
1 pound mushrooms of your choice
2 tablespoons olive oil
Pacific Rim Noodle House Black Bean Sauce

Chop the bok choy into bite-sized pieces.
Chop mushrooms separately.
In a sauté pan over medium-high heat, pour olive oil. Add chopped bok choy and stir-fry until wilted, about two minutes.
Add mushrooms and stir-fry 2 minutes.
Remove from heat.
Dress with black bean sauce and serve.
(4 side dish servings)

Recipe courtesy of Carol Davis, Pacific Rim Noodle House, Arcata

The fritters, with generous chunks of shrimp and crab meat, sparked by Sweet Mama Janisse's Soy-Gin Sauce, would be great alone, but the tang of Pacific Rim Noodle House Chile-Lime Sauce is the perfect accompaniment for the richness of the crab.

Seafood Fritters with Chile-Lime Sauce

    3 garlic cloves
    1 tablespoon minced fresh ginger
    3 tablespoons lime juice
    3 tablespoons Sweet Mama Janisse's Soy-Gin Sauce
    2 eggs
    1/4 cup flour
    8 ounces crabmeat, drained and patted dry with a paper towel
    8 ounces cooked shrimp, chopped
    1/4 cup cilantro, finely chopped
    1/4 cup roasted red bell pepper, chopped
    vegetable oil
    mixed baby greens
    Pacific Rim Noodle House Chile-Lime Sauce

In a mixing bowl, beat garlic, ginger, lime juice, Sweet Mama Janisse's Soy-Gin Sauce, and the eggs until thoroughly blended.

Beat in flour, mixing well.

Mix in crab, shrimp, cilantro and red bell peppers. Set aside.

In a large, heavy skillet over medium-high heat, add a one-inch layer of oil and heat to 350 degrees F.

Drop heaping tablespoons of the seafood batter into the hot oil. Cook about three minutes. Flip, and cook two to three minutes more. Drain on paper towels.

Place mixed baby greens on each of four salad plates. Top with fritters. Fill individual sauce cups with Pacific Rim Noodle House Chile-Lime Sauce for dipping, and serve.

(4 first course servings)

Carol shares the basic recipe. Feel free to create your own variations. Avocado, bay shrimp, crab meat, scrambled eggs, sweet corn or tofu, would work well in this quick-fix.

Vegetable Quesadilla
    4 flour tortillas
    1 cup diced tomatoes
    1 cup chopped onion
    1 cup shredded Jack cheese
    sour cream
    mixed baby greens

Warm tortillas in an oven until soft. Remove from heat.
Fill with tomatoes, onions and jack cheese.
Top with sour cream and Pacific Rim Noodle House Black Bean Sauce.
Fold in half.
Place a bed of baby greens on each plate. Top with two folded quesadillas.
(2 servings, 2 quesadillas each)

Recipe courtesy of Carol Davis, Pacific Rim Noodle House, Arcata

Marie states emphatically that she's a cook, not a chef. Watching her work, one senses an instinctive understanding to the way ingredients work together. Yet she insists that her recipes are not carved in stone, and she encourages others to adjust them up or down according to personal taste.

Louisiana French Dressing

2 cups canola oil
1 cup olive oil
3 Tablespoons Worcestershire sauce
1 Tablespoon salt
2 Tablespoons sugar
6 cloves garlic, minced
½ cup green onions, minced (white and green parts)
1/4 cup minced parsley

Mix all ingredients together and beat (or run through a blender) until an emulsion results.

Store leftovers, tightly covered, in refrigerator.

(3 ½ cups salad dressing)

Recipe courtesy of Marie Wilkins, Sweet Mama Janisse Products and Bless My Soul Café, Eureka

Marijuana © *Matthew Filar*

CHAPTER EIGHT

CASH CROP

People nationwide know Southern Humboldt for its cash crop. In a book by the same name, author Ray Raphael details the marijuana industry and its impact on the area. The book is a small masterpiece, written with no apparent bias other than an obvious intent to put to rest the media hype.

Major periodicals such as *Time* and *Esquire* have come to see what the fuss was all about. Television networks and newspapers as widely respected as *The New York Times* have sent reporters to cover the story of the new "gold in them thar hills." All too often the reports that resulted focused not on the full picture, but on the seamiest isolated details. Raphael's self-stated purpose was to present a fuller, clearer picture.

In fact, the area *has* come under the economic influence of growers large and small since the late sixties. Depressed land prices drew back-to-the-landers in record numbers, and more often than not they opted to include *cannabis sativa* seeds in their garden plots. Because of the rural nature of the area, the small, private-use "grows" went largely unnoticed at first.

Gradually, however, the potential for profit became apparent, and a shift occurred in the demographics. What once resembled the Garden of Eden became more like a war zone as armed guards and elaborate security systems on the ground came under attack by helicopters in the air, manned by Campaign Against Marijuana Propagation (C.A.M.P.). Here, one frequently notices bumper stickers proclaiming "Get U.S. out of Humboldt County."

In 1996, California voters passed Proposition 215, making marijuana available to patients with prescriptions. Humboldt County District Attorney Paul Gallegos ran on a campaign which, among other things, pledged his support to the initiative, despite the federal government's resistance. He unseated the long-entrenched incumbent, but the road has not been without potholes. In 2004, he faced, and won, a recall election. But the future for 215 patients is still not out of the woods, and so far, during the growing season, the helicopters still fly.

In the midst of it all, in the heart of Garberville, a town of about two thousand people, Pam Hanson runs a small breakfast/lunch spot called The Woodrose Café. Hanson moved to Garberville from Cleveland, Ohio, in the early nineteen seventies. In 1977, when Herb's Café appeared on the real estate market, her parents, Woodrose and Amy Hanson bought it for her. In appreciation, she changed the name to honor her father. "I didn't know anything about cooking," she admits. "I still don't. But I loved food, and I loved people."

Herb's had been a Mexican restaurant. "Before that, it was Bud's," Hanson says, smiling at the fact that both names are commonly used to refer to the crop that put Southern Humboldt on the map. "I started making changes gradually at first. I offered buckwheat pancakes because I remembered them as being homey and old-fashioned. And I switched from artificially flavored maple syrup to the pure stuff."

Many of the area's newcomers at the time were already seeking a more natural lifestyle, so the changes found a ready welcome. And as organic foods became increasingly available, Hanson added them to the menu. " I could have gone vegetarian, but my father insisted that to be successful a breakfast menu had to offer bacon and sausage." So she went for the best: Niman Ranch bacon and Humboldt Sausage Company's chicken-apple sausage. "I get a lot of my products locally," she says with obvious satisfaction. "We use Casa Lindra salsas, Humboldt Creamery dairy products, and tofu from The Tofu Shop in Arcata.

The customers love it. The restaurant is usually crowded, with the clientele spilling over onto the patio in good weather. Hanson needs to do very little advertising. "Word of mouth is always the best," she maintains. "Nobody says 'I used this great dry cleaner last week.' But they talk about restaurants."

The staff is equally loyal. Chef Bill Staples has run the kitchen since 1982, Tracy Shapiro has waited tables since 1994, and Hanson's brother Tom has kept the books and worked behind the counter since they opened.

"I had a lot of jobs before I got here," Hanson says. "I drove a cab. I did strip tease. I did all kinds of things, and I had all kinds of bosses. Some were nice. Some weren't. I've tried to be the kind of boss I enjoyed working for.

"I'd never been a boss before, and when we opened, it was mostly a family operation. Then one day a young girl, a college student, came in looking for a job. I didn't even have any applications, and I'd never conducted a job interview. I actually asked her, 'What's your sign?'"

Among her most memorable guests she counts Angela Davis and Joan Baez. "And we had a woman from New York. She was out on the patio having breakfast. As I walked by I heard her say, 'I can't believe it. Blintzes in the middle of nowhere!'

"I always wanted this to be one of the best restaurants anywhere in the world," she says. "A restaurant is more than food. It's personality. I'm grateful for this community." She pauses to look around at the people – all ages, all sorts, interacting with the wait staff and with each other with obvious good nature – and she smiles again.

"Someone once referred to this place as the heartbeat of Southern Humboldt," she recalls. "I like that a lot."

Down Garberville's main street, a block and a half from the café, The Hemp Connection retails clothing and paper products crafted from the multifunctional fibers of the *cannabis sativa* plant. Environmentalists widely tout its potential commercial uses, especially in the face of what they see as the vanishing forests throughout the county. They are quick to point out that Thomas Jefferson grew hemp and encouraged others to grow it as well, calling the plant a necessity. In 1930, some say, Henry Ford made motorcars from hemp, painted them with hemp paint and fueled them with hemp fuel. In fact, the federal government did not ban the growing of hemp until 1937, and the American Medical Association openly opposed that decision at the time.

The Hemp Connection functions legally, but its relationship to the illegal substance is hardly subtle. In Southern Humboldt, pot fuels the economy and virtually everyone knows it, but in most businesses, the connection is harder to pin down. Hardware and farm supply stores are not required to ask how the merchandise they sell will be used. The auto dealer who sells a pick-up truck for cash is under no obligation to find out where that cash came from.

Since the advent of C.A.M.P. helicopters, many large-scale operations have moved indoors. The resulting product is called "diesel dope" because of the diesel-powered generators used to produce it. Excessive use of electricity sends a red flag to the power company; diesel generators do not. Unfortunately, indoor "grows" are subject to mite infestations and must be chemically treated. Thus, the end result no longer strictly qualifies as organic.

Southern Humboldt natives Lon and Laney remember how it was "before the hips came." Life had taken them to the San Francisco Bay Area for a time, but when their children were born in the nineteen sixties, they decided to return to their roots.

"Potlucks were the big thing," Laney recalls. "We were always having potlucks, and of course everyone always brought their best recipes. Artichokes, crab, salmon, and abalone. Can you imagine abalone chowder?" Her eyes light up at the recollection.

"And of course, everyone visited everyone else. We were all really close – like family. You could tell how folks were doing when you went to their homes. The people who were doing well always put on a spread. The people having a harder time served cheese and crackers.

"Everyone had a garden, and we always had venison. I think the game warden looked the other way if he knew you were using deer meat to feed your family. I used to put the meat in tomato sauce or barbecue sauce I made and can it up real quick so I could hide it on the shelf, though, just in case. We always told the kids it was 'side-gill salmon' or 'valley lamb.' I remember once we got invited to an event where venison was served. One of the kids said, 'Gosh, Mom. Deer meat tastes just like valley lamb.'"

"This is the real West," Lon adds. "It has a deep, rich history. In the eighteen sixties, the only way to get stuff here was by boat to Shelter Cove, then from there by stage to Briceland. Briceland was a thriving community. Whatever people needed that wasn't already here had to come through Briceland."

Today, Highway 101 will get you from San Francisco to Garberville in about five hours. People and goods flow in and out of the area smoothly. Each summer, for example, Reggae on the River, a non-profit music festival, turns Southern Humboldt upside down. Thousands of dreadlocked fans descend on the Eel River at French's Camp in tiny Piercy for three days of what has been called "indisputably the best reggae music festival in the world."

Ironically – or maybe not– Reggae is a musical expression of the Rastafarian movement. Its followers, in many ways like the hippies who came to Southern Humboldt decades earlier, have looked at the world around them and said, in effect, "That doesn't work." They have adopted hairstyles and lifestyles which set them apart from the status quo and delight in the difference. "Ganja" (marijuana) is, quite literally, the sacrament of their faith.

In Eureka, Shawn Whelihan grows his own. He's been eligible to do so since 1999. "I really wasn't motivated, but a friend put me on the waiting list to see the pot clinic's doctor. That was just the push I needed," he explains. He had no trouble obtaining the prescription he needed to legitimize his horticultural efforts. A long-standing knee injury made him a likely candidate. But the satisfaction he draws from the process of growing his remedy is healing in itself.

"My pot's pretty good," he says modestly "I really think it's because I grow it with a lot of love." It takes a lot of work too, though. "I grow outdoors in a greenhouse in mild weather. I have to clear the soil, bring in new soil, dig in the amendments, all of your basic gardening. The plants are easy targets for spider mites and a little green worm – I'm not sure what it's called. But I don't use any pesticides. I don't want to end up smoking that stuff. Besides, there's plenty to go around. Even with the bugs, I harvest all I need.

"The rest of the year I have an indoor grow. I use my closet. I've put all my clothes in another room, and I've set up a hydroponic system in my bedroom. I use a six hundred watt grow bulb, and grow the plants in rock wool. Because there's no soil involved, I have to add a lot of nutrients. And after the first few weeks, I test the pH every night and adjust the nutrients if necessary."

When he harvests, he hangs the plants on hooks in his bedroom walls for about a week. "It gets a little skunky," he admits. As it dries, he trims it removing any extraneous stems and leaves, and packs it into mason jars. Using a vacuum sealer, he extracts the air from the jars and tightens the rings to maintain freshness. "I guess it's just like canning fish or game or anything else.

So no matter what the weather, I've got what I need."

Empathetic by nature, he spends time talking to his plants, certain that his emotional input benefits them. "If I cook a meal when I feel good, when I'm happy, then it goes together smoothly and everyone who shares it with me comments on how good it is. If I cook when I'm angry or upset, the result is totally different. "I figure it's the same with my gardening. I'm putting out energy, and the plants are picking that energy up. Since in the end I'm going to smoke, or eat, or drink the substance of those plants, I want them to be the best I can help them be. So I put the best that I have into tending them.

"Not often, but once in a while I cook with it. What I notice is that when I smoke it, it goes to my head. When I eat it, it goes to my body."

Further north, in Arcata, Native American Vietnam veteran Robert (Standing Bear) LaFrance holds the distinction of having not one, but two prescriptions for medical marijuana. When doctors first began to write script in the nineteen nineties, friends took him to a facility where qualified patients could obtain a physician's authorization.

"The doctor turned out to be a man I had some history with," he says. "When I would visit friends at the Veterans' Hospital in San Francisco, I would see him there. He'd walk by and patients would call out to him as if he was a friend they were glad to see. That was pretty unusual.

"Anyhow, I walked into the clinic and we recognized each other. When I told him I'd like to get a prescription, he said, 'No problem.' He sat down and started writing. I was kind of surprised, but he said he knew me and that I had post traumatic stress disorder from being in Vietnam. I said, 'I don't think I have that.' He just said, 'Yes, you do,' and smiled at me.

"Later I was arrested, and the police said that this doctor wrote too many prescriptions for pot and they wouldn't honor mine. I'd have to go to court. So I went to my regular doctor and told her my problem. She said that she'd written a prescription for me months earlier for my arthritis, but she hadn't given it to me because I'd never asked for it. She picked up my file, took out the prescription and handed it to me.

"I took the two prescriptions to court and showed them to the judge. She ruled that since the two doctors concurred, my need for medical marijuana was not merely a medical opinion but an established medical fact. Because of some earlier problems I had I'm not allowed to grow it or live where it's being grown, but people can grow it for me, or give it to me, or sell it to me, and I can use it legally.

"Before I got this, they had prescribed valium, vicodin, amitryptolene and paxil. All those drugs have side effects that I don't want to deal with. For me, the herb takes care of it all.

"My grandfather used it for years. He used to make what he called 'herbal decoctions' in various combinations depending on what was needed. He made poultices, salves, syrups, all kinds of herbal remedies, and pot was often an essential ingredient.

"Smoking pot is the quickest way to get the benefit, but there are lots of different ways to use it. When I eat it, it takes a little longer to feel the effects, but the results last longer.

"I like to make pastries with it. I'll use oils or put it in butter and use it to make apple strudel, cinnamon rolls, apple crumb cakes or apple crisp. When my wife was dying from cancer, I used to put it in everything I fixed for her. Spaghetti, rice, eggs.... I used to fix red snapper. I'd cook it in oil, then put a little pot butter on it. We ate a lot of snapper.

"She couldn't eat much. Between the cancer and the drugs they gave her, she had no appetite, and when she did eat, food would make her sick. I'd cook her vegetables in water, and then put a little pot butter on top. She'd eat that." While proponents claim that marijuana will alleviate the symptoms of cancer, no one promotes it as a cure. LaFrance's wife passed on very shortly after the birth of their fifth child in 1990. He still misses her, but he is grateful that he was able to be with her and ease her suffering up to the end.

The clinic where he got his first prescription, The Humboldt Patient Resource Center currently operates out a modest building in an Arcata neighborhood where residential and commercial structures overlap. It is established as a limited liability corporation which functions to serve the needs of people who hold prescriptions for medical marijuana.

The knowledgeable young woman behind the desk handles her fast-paced job with calm and pleasant assurance. She answers phones, makes referrals, pulls files, and acknowledges walk-ins simultaneously without missing a beat. "As a proposition 215 clinic, we try to maintain a relatively low profile, but we provide a lot of services to people who're qualified. We help settle landlord disputes. We help people get funding. We assist people returning to school. The owner is a sociologist, so he's always encouraging people to go back to school."

Practically speaking, qualification simply means being in possession of a prescription for marijuana written by a licensed California physician. Filling the prescription – which won't happen at your local pharmacy – is another service the Center provides. A whiteboard next to the access window announces that currently the clinic has on hand a variety of marijuana referred to as "Train Wreck." Under the announcement, a list testifies to other varieties expected to arrive in the near future along with the anticipated delivery dates.

Linda Ann, the receptionist, goes on to explain that, as of this writing, in California (which is legally at odds with current federal statutes) if a doctor prescribes marijuana for a specific medical condition, you can grow and personally use a specifically limited quantity of the plant.

Current guidelines established in Humboldt County by the District Attorney specify for outdoor cultivation:

Patients or their caregivers cultivating marijuana in an area within one hundred (100) square feet cumulatively measured by the vegetative canopy of the plants and who have ninety-nine (99) plants or less, including starts, shall be deemed within the District Attorney's prosecution guidelines and will not be prosecuted.

For indoor cultivation, those same guidelines state:

Patients or their caregivers cultivating marijuana in an area within one hundred (100) square feet cumulatively measured by the vegetative canopy of the plants and who have ninety-nine (99) plants or less including starts, and who are using one and one-half (1.5) kilowatts (1500 watts) or less of illumination by artificial growing lights of any kind shall be deemed within the District Attorney's prosecution guidelines and will not be prosecuted.

Even with the passing of the initiative and the District Attorney's clear guidelines, many physicians are reluctant to prescribe medical marijuana. The Center offers assistance here as well by arranging appointments with a doctor willing to prescribe for patients whose conditions warrant use of the plant. Those conditions may be physical, such as cancer or glaucoma; they may be psychological, such as depression or post traumatic stress disorder. The symptoms users feel marijuana alleviates form a broad spectrum.

Not everyone can – or chooses to – smoke. At the center, Linda Ann says, "We encourage patients to ingest. We even hand out recipes. Probably the easiest way is to make it into 'cannabutter.' Then just substitute it for the butter in any recipe.

"I make it into flour, too. I just dry it and use a blender to turn it into a powder. Then I run it through a fine sieve to remove any grit or other foreign matter that might be there and substitute it for up to a third of the flour the recipe calls for."

Perhaps the best known use of marijuana in cooking is "Alice B. Toklas Brownies." The story surrounding that recipe is this: Toklas had a contract to produce a cookbook. As her deadline grew near, she realized she needed more recipes and sent out an S.O.S. to her friends. One friend sent her a recipe calling for marijuana as a joke, but the author, pressed for time, included it with the others without bothering to read it.

In fact, the recipe produced nothing like brownies as we know them. It was a concoction of dried fruits and nuts, dusted with spices and ground cannabis, well-kneaded with butter and sugar and shaped into small balls or cut into squares. Quite possibly, the end result was delicious, but for a true chocolate lover it would never live up to expectations.

Whatever their intentions, the disenchanted youth of the sixties who fled to Southern Humboldt could not have foreseen the impact their influx would have on the future of their new homeland or on the state of California as a whole.

The recipes below are included because this book is about what people eat in Humboldt County. They are not intended for use by anyone not legally permitted to use them, and should never, NEVER, be served to anyone without their full awareness of the ingredients involved.

NORTH COAST WAYS WITH HERB-LACED FOODS

The following recipe is given as it was received. Since the butter will keep almost indefinitely in the refrigerator if it's well-wrapped, many people find it more practical to prepare a pound or more at a time. Simply increase both ingredients in equal proportions.

Nurse Deborah's Butter Recipe for Patients in Distress

   1/4 ounce of Bud   (dried marijuana buds)

- OR -

   3/4 ounce of shake (leaves of the plant - less potent)

   1/4 pound of butter (1 stick)

   Cook in a crock pot or double boiler on low for eight to twelve hours.

   Strain through cheese cloth. You may wish to use a very little boiling water to rinse out the last of the "green stuff", but make sure it's very little.

   Toss out the "green stuff."

   Use the butter in cooking in any recipe, brownies, garlic bread, anything that calls for butter.

   (1/4 pound)

   Recipe courtesy of The Humboldt Patient Resource Center, Arcata

These are brownies the way we're used to them, but with the bonus of added symptom relievers. Use the darkest, richest cocoa powder you can find for optimum flavor.

Forget Alice's Brownies
   ½ cup "canna" butter
   ½ cup cocoa powder
   1 cup granulated sugar
   2 eggs
   1 tablespoon vanilla
   ½ cup flour
   1/4 teaspoon salt
   ½ cup chopped nuts, if desired

Preheat oven to 350 degrees F.

Grease an 8"x8"x2" baking dish. Set aside.

In a saucepan over low heat, melt the butter.

Stir in the cocoa powder, mixing well.

Stir in the sugar, mixing thoroughly.

Remove from heat.

Beat the eggs into the mixture, one at a time, beating well after each addition.

Add the vanilla, mixing well.

Add the flour and salt, stirring just enough to blend thoroughly. Be careful not to over beat.

Pour the batter into the prepared pan. Bake twenty-five to thirty minutes, until a toothpick, inserted into the center of the pan comes out clean.

(16 2 ½" x 2 ½" brownies)

This is another basic way to get marijuana into recipes easily. Because heat can destroy the potency of marijuana, and this method requires no heat, it is quite effective. Used in salad dressings, it has no exposure to heat at all.

Bear Oil

1 generous handful of dried leaves and stems, well broken up

- OR -

half that amount of bud

2 cups of oil of your choice (olive, canola, vegetable, whatever)

In a clean, dry jar with a screw-top lid, place the vegetable matter.
Pour the oil into the jar, tighten the lid and give it a few good shakes.
Store in a warm, dark place for a week, shaking it from time to time.
Strain the oil through cheesecloth into a fresh jar, and cap.
Use in any recipe that calls for oil.
(1 pint of oil)

Recipe courtesy of Standing Bear, Arcata

This recipe takes a favorite hors d'euvre and transforms it into a way to help your patient feel it's a special celebration.

Chrissie's Magic Mushrooms
1/4 cup "canna" butter
1 small onion, finely chopped
1 rib of celery, finely chopped
2 dozen mushrooms
garlic salt to taste
basil to taste
Italian seasoning to taste
4 ounces cream cheese
½ cup bread crumbs
1/4 cup grated Parmesan cheese
cooking spray

Preheat oven to 400 degrees F.
In a medium skillet, melt butter over medium heat.
Add onion and celery and cook, stirring as needed.
Chop mushroom stems, reserving caps. Add stems to skillet. Stir all till the vegetables are soft. Add seasonings and cream cheese, stirring till cheese melts and the mix is well-blended. Remove from heat and stir in the bread crumbs and Parmesan cheese.
Spray a large baking sheet with cooking spray. Stuff reserved mushroom caps with skillet mixture and place on baking sheet.
Bake fifteen minutes, until golden brown.
(24 mushrooms)

Recipe courtesy of a friend

Because caregivers are often pressed for time, convenience foods are greatly appreciated. The following recipe utilizes them in a manner I'm told is not only effective but tasty as well. "Ganja" is an especially potent form of marijuana.

Ganja Lasagna

1 package oven ready lasagna

1 pound ground beef, or an equivalent amount of TVP

1 25-ounce jar spaghetti sauce

1 cup water

½ cup plus 1/4 cup grated Parmesan cheese

1 tablespoon dried grated Ganja buds

1 pound ricotta cheese

½ pound mozzarella cheese, grated

salt and pepper to taste

1 egg, beaten

2 cups spinach

a dash of nutmeg

Preheat oven to 375 degrees F.

In a saucepan, brown ground beef. Drain off fat. Add spaghetti sauce and water and bring to a boil. Reserve ½ cup of the Parmesan cheese. In a large bowl mix together 1/4 cup of the Parmesan and remaining ingredients.

In a 13"x9"x2" baking dish spread 1/3 of the meat sauce. Layer with ½ the lasagna, ½ the cheese mixture, 1/3 of the meat sauce, remaining pasta, remaining cheese and the remaining sauce. Top with reserved Parmesan, cover pan with aluminum foil, and bake forty minutes. Uncover and bake fifteen minutes more. Remove from oven and let stand five to ten minutes before cutting.

Yields 6 to 8 servings

Recipe courtesy of The Humboldt Patient Resource Center

This is presented as a side dish. Actually, it has many uses. It's good, warmed and served over pancakes or waffles at breakfast. It's equally good over ice cream any time of the day. It will even brighten a bowl of oatmeal.

Little Green Apples

    1/3 cup "canna" butter
    1 large orange, zested and juiced
    1/3 cup granulated sugar
    2 teaspoons cinnamon
    1/4 teaspoon ground cloves
    2 Granny Smith apples, peeled, cored and cut into wedges

In a medium saucepan over low heat, melt butter.

Stir in the orange juice, 1 tablespoon of the orange zest, sugar, cinnamon and cloves. Cook, stirring, till sugar dissolves and the syrup is well blended.

Add the sliced apples. Stir to coat each wedge thoroughly with the syrup. Cover and cook, stirring frequently, until the apples are tender, but not mushy, ten to fifteen minutes.

Remove from heat. Serve immediately, or cool to room temperature, cover and refrigerate.

Yields 2 side servings

Recipe courtesy of a friend

This cornbread recipe is spicy in more ways than one. Heat may be reduced (or eliminated) by adjusting down the jalapenos.

Down Home Corn Muffins

1/4 cup "canna" butter
2 eggs, well beaten
½ cup minced onion
1 cup cornmeal
1 teaspoon salt
½ teaspoon baking soda
1 cup milk
1 cup cream-style corn
3 tablespoons minced jalapenos
1 cup grated sharp cheddar cheese.

Preheat oven to 400 degrees F.
Grease muffin tins for eighteen two-inch muffins.
Melt the "canna" butter over low heat. Remove immediately.
In a mixing bowl, combine ingredients, one at a time, stirring well after each addition.
Using a 1/4 cup measure, place batter into tins.
Bake thirty minutes.

Yields 18 two-inch muffins

Popeye never had it so good. The bright green of fresh spinach, the rich red of the peppers, and the pale gold of the Swiss cheese make it as good to look at as it is to eat.

Spinach au Gratin with Roasted Red Bell Peppers

2 10-ounce bags baby spinach
2 tablespoons "canna" butter
2 tablespoons Bear Oil
1 large leek, white part only, thinly sliced
1 small shallot, minced
2 cloves garlic, minced
½ cup half and half
2 large eggs
½ cup ricotta cheese
½ cup grated Swiss cheese
salt and pepper to taste
2 roasted red bell peppers, peeled, seeded, and cut into narrow strips

Preheat oven to 350 degrees F.

In a large skillet over medium-high heat, quickly cook spinach, a batch at a time, until it wilts. Drain, and press between towels to squeeze out excess moisture.

In a large skillet over medium heat, melt butter.

Add oil to heat.

Add leek, shallot and garlic, and cook four to five minutes, until vegetables are soft. Remove from heat. Stir in the spinach and 2/3 of the pepper strips. Set aside.

In a large mixing bowl, using a whisk, thoroughly blend cream with eggs.

Add ricotta, 2/3 of the Swiss cheese, salt and pepper, mixing well.

Stir in spinach mixture.

Pour into a well-greased 9" baking dish. Bake thirty to thirty-five minutes.

Remove from oven and sprinkle remaining Swiss cheese evenly over the top.

Return to the oven and bake until cheese melts.

Garnish with remaining pepper strips and serve.

Yields 4 servings

Great Egret Arcata Marsh   © Matthew Filar

DIRECTORY

Legend: $ = $5.00 - $15.00
                $$ = $15.00 - $25.00
              $$$ = $25.00 or more

Avalon
3rd and G Streets
Eureka, 95501
(707) 445-0500
Lunch, Dinner, Full Service Bar, Innovative Menu $$$
www.avaloneureka.com

Alex Begovic, Chef/Caterer
130 Cedar Street
Eureka, 95501
(707) 476-9369

Bless My Soul Café
29 5th Street
Eureka, 95501
(707) 443-1090
Dinner Tuesday - Thursday 5:00-9:00 p.m.
Friday & Saturday 5:00-10:00 p.m.
Soul Food, Creole-Style, Wine & Beer,
Sweet Mama Janisse's Sauces $
 www.sweetmamajanisse.com

Briceland Vineyards Winery
5959 Briceland-Shelter Cove Road
Redway , 95542
(707) 923-2429
Award-Winning Wines

My Time Ranch
Humboldt Hill Road
Eureka, 95503
Award-winning chevre
www.capriciouscheese.com

Carter House, Hotel Carter, Restaurant 301
301 L Street
Eureka, 95501
(707) 444-8062
Bed and Breakfast Accommodations,
Fine Dining, Award-Winning Wine List $$$
www.carterhouse.com

Curley's Grill
400 Ocean Avenue
Ferndale, 95536
(707) 786-9696
Lunch and Dinner, Something for Everyone,
Full Service Bar, $$

Cypress Grove Chevre
4600 Dows Prairie Road
McKinleyville, 95519
(707) 839-3168
Fine Goat Cheeses
www.cypressgrovechevre.com

Eel River Brewing Company
1777 Alamar Way
Fortuna, 95540
(707) 725-2739
Lunch and Dinner, Pub Fare
award-winning Micro-brews $
www.climaxbeer.com

Fieldbrook Valley Winery
4242 Fieldbrook Road
Fieldbrook 95519
(707) 839-4140
Award-Winning Wines
www.fieldbrookwinery.com

Folie Douce
1551 G Street
Arcata, 95521
(707) 822-1042
Dinner Tuesday-Thursday 5:30-9:00 p.m.
Friday & Saturday 5:30 - 10:00 p.m.
Innovative Menu, Extensive Wine List $$$
www. holyfolie.com

Gills by the Bay
77 Halibut Avenue
Eureka, 95503
(707) 442-2554
Opens daily at 6:00 a.m.
Breakfast and Lunch, Fresh Seafood $

Gingerbread Mansion Inn
400 Berding Street
Ferndale, 95536
(707) 786-4000
Award-Winning Bed and Breakfast Accommodations
Reservation Number - (800) 952-4136
www. gingerbreadmansion.com

Hoopa Processing Corporation
Hoopa Reservation
Hoopa 95573
(530) 625-4389
Indian-Kippered Wild Salmon
HPChoopa@yahoo.com

Humboldt Bay Mycological Society
P.O. Box 4419
Arcata, 95518
Meetings September through May, third Wednesdays
3471 Jacoby Creek Road, Bayside 7:30 p.m.
Foraging one Saturday each month, To Be Announced

Hurricane Kate's
511 Second Street
Eureka, 95501
(707) 444-1405
Lunch and Dinner Tuesday through Saturday
"Whirled Fusion Cuisine," Full-Service Bar $$

The Jambalaya
915 H Street
Arcata, 95521
(707) 822-4766
Tuesday- Saturday 5:00 p.m. - 9:00 p.m.
American Bistro Featuring Robust, Full-Flavored
Seasonal Cuisine, Full-Service Bar $$$

Larrupin Café
1658 Patricks Point Drive
Trinidad 95570
(707) 677-0230
Dinner Tuesday through Saturday
Innovative Menu, Full-Service Bar,
al fresco Dining Option $$$

The Lost Whale
3452 Patricks Point Drive
Trinidad, 95570
(707) 677-3425
Bed and Breakfast Accommodations
Reservation Number - (800) 677-7859

Lazio Family Products
2907 F Street
Eureka, 95501
(707) 442-3767
Gourmet Albacore
www.laziotuna.com

Loleta Cheese Factory
292 Loleta Drive
Loleta, 95551
(707) 733-5470
Open Daily, Award-Winning Cheeses,
Gourmet Food Products and Gifts
www.loletacheesefactory.com

Lost Coast Brewery and Café
617 Fourth Street
Eureka, 95501
(707) 445-4480
Sunday to Wednesday 11:00a.m.- midnight
Thursday - Saturday   11:00 a.m. - 1:00 a.m.
Pub Fare, award-wining Micro-Brews, $
www.lostcoast.com

Lluvia Winery
4185 Bush Avenue
Mckinleyville, CA 95519
(707) 840-0705
dcgray@northcoast.com

Moonstone Grill
100 Moonstone Beach Road
Trinidad, 95570
(707) 677-1616
An Evening of Fine Dining in Breathtaking Surroundings, $$$

Pacific Rim Noodle House
1021 I Street
Arcata, 95521
(707) 826-7604
"A California Spin on the Pacific Rim"
Monday - Saturday 11:00 a.m. to 7:00 p.m.
Healthy, flavorful, light food on site or to go;
Pacific Rim Noodle House Sauces; $
www.pacificrimnoodle.com

Potters Produce
106 Buckley Road
Blue Lake, 95525
(707) 668-5387
Pumpkin Patch and Corn Maze in October

Sjaak's Fine Belgian Chocolates
425 Snug Alley
Eureka, 95501
(707) 445-0326
Wholesale, Retail, Custom Ordering (800) 869-6506

Reed's Bees
911 Bayview
Arcata, 95521
(707) 826-1744
Honeys, Beeswax Candles

Rolf's Park Café
Highway 101 at Davidson Road
Orick, 95555
(707) 488-3841
German and American Food, Seafood and Game $$

The Tofu Shop Specialty Foods, Inc.
65 Frank Martin Court
Arcata 95521
(707) 822-7401
Tofu Products, Soy Milk
www.tofushop.com

Tomaso's Specialty Foods
P.O. Box 908
Blue Lake, 95525
(707) 668-1868
Italian Sauces and Pestos made by hand

Wolfsen Farms
2103 Baird Road
McKinleyville, 95519
(707) 839-2017
"You Pick" Blueberries by appointment in July and August

The Woodrose Café
911 Redwood Drive
Garberville, 95542
(707) 923-3191
Breakfast Monday through Friday 8:00 a.m. to noon
Saturday and Sunday 8:00 a.m. to 1:00 p.m.
Lunch Monday through Friday noon to 2:30 p.m.
Fresh organic food deliciously prepared $

CALENDAR OF EVENTS

A tremendous benefit of isolation: You learn to make your own fun. Humboldt County does it well. Historically, our fun has centered around food. From Native American salmon feasts, to pioneer potlucks, to pancake breakfasts and spaghetti dinners today, we party with food. Some of the annual food-related shindigs here include the following:

A Taste of Main Street - Eureka   *March*

Bebop and Brew - Arcata   *June*

Trinidad Fish and Art Festival   *June*

Art and Wine in the Park - Fortuna   *June*

Chili Cook-off - Willow Creek   *June*

Westhaven Blackberry Festival   *July*

Fortuna Food and Fun   *September*

Tastes of Ferndale and Friends   *September*

Elders Dinner Salmon Feast – Eureka   *September*

Apple Harvest Festival - Fortuna   *October*

Mushroom Fair - Eureka   *November*

Taste of the Holidays - Arcata   *November*

We also celebrate on a grand scale throughout the year. These are some of the events that draw people from all over the world:

March - Redwood Coast Dixieland Jazz Festival

April - Godwit Days

May - Kinetic Sculpture Race

June - Arcata Bay Oyster Festival

July - Blues by the Bay

August - Reggae on the River

For information on any of these events, contact:
Humboldt County Convention and Visitors Bureau
1034 Second Street
Eureka, CA 95501
(800) 346 - 3482
www.redwoodvisitor.org

Trillium Falls   © *Matthew Filar*